# CHRISTIAN VALUES AND VIRTUES

## Other Works by the Editor

*Becoming Community: Biblical Meditations and Applications in Modern Life.* Hyde Park, N.Y.: New City Press, 2007.

*How to Pray with the Bible.* Huntington, Ind.: Our Sunday Visitor, 2007.

*The Bible and You,* with Loreen Hanley Duquin. Huntington, Ind.: Our Sunday Visitor, 2004.

*The How-To Book of the Bible.* Huntington, Ind.: Our Sunday Visitor, 2004.

*Calming the Stormy Seas of Stress.* Winona, Minn.: St. Mary's Press, 1998.

*Job Therapy.* Pittsburgh, Pa.: Genesis Personal Development Center, 1996.

*Journaling with Moses and Job.* Boston: St. Paul Books and Media, 1996.

*Personal Energy Manager Rainbow Planner.* Pittsburgh, Pa.: Genesis Personal Development Center, 1996.

*The Art and Vocation of Caring for Persons in Pain.* Mahwah, N.J.: Paulist Press, 1994.

*Nourished by the Word,* with Andrew Campbell, O.S.B. Notre Dame, Ind.: Ave Maria Press, 1994.

*Personal Energy Management: A Christian Personal and Professional Development Program.* Chicago: Loyola University Press, 1994.

*Where Is God When You Need Him? Sharing Stories of Suffering with Job and Jesus.* Staten Island, N.Y.: Alba House, 1992.

# CHRISTIAN VALUES AND VIRTUES

## POPE PAUL VI

EDITED AND INTRODUCED BY
KARL A. SCHULTZ

*A Crossroad Book*
The Crossroad Publishing Company
New York

The Crossroad Publishing Company
16 Penn Plaza – 481 Eighth Avenue, Suite 1550
New York, NY 10001

Printed in the United States of America on acid-free paper

The text of this book is set in 10/13 Cheltenham and 10/13 Optima. The display face is Cheltenham.

**Library of Congress Cataloging-in-Publication Data**

Christian values and virtues / edited by Karl A. Schultz.
    p.  cm.
    Includes bibliographical references.
    ISBN-13: 978-0-8245-2450-0 (alk. paper)
    ISBN-10: 0-8245-2450-0 (alk. paper)
    1. Paul VI, Pope, 1897-1978 – Quotations. 2. Catholic Church – Doctrines. I. Paul VI, Pope, 1897-1978. II. Schultz, Karl A., 1959- III. Title.
    BX1378.3.C47 2006
    282.092 – dc22
    [B]

                                2006035297

1  2  3  4  5  6  7  8  9  10      12  11  10  09  08  07

*To Mom and Dad,*
*for supporting me in my*
*life, faith, growth, and business*

# Contents

*Chapter 1*

# The Life and Legacy of Pope Paul VI

Giovanni Battista Enrico Antonio Maria Montini was born on September 26, 1897, into a prominent and devout Catholic family. He was a precocious youth who exhibited many of the qualities that would characterize his adult life: a remarkable memory, an elusive reserve often mistaken as coldness, a natural and developed ability as a writer and wordsmith, a devotion to study, an admiration of culture and literature, and a lack of enthusiasm for superficial pursuits. He was sickly for much of his youth, and there was concern that his ill health would interfere with his priestly ministry.

His father, Giorgio, was a prominent Italian lawyer, publisher, and activist. His mother, Giuditta, was extensively involved in Catholic social work and activism. His elder brother was an attorney and politician, his younger brother a doctor. He grew up in a staunchly Catholic province in Italy called Brescia.

Giovanni Montini was ordained a priest on May 19, 1920. His pre-diplomatic priestly service left him with a great understanding and affection for workers, youth, and the poor. In tandem with Monsignor Domenico Tardini he operated as Pope Pius XII's secretary of state from 1939 through 1954, when he became archbishop of Milan. He was made a cardinal by Pope John XXIII in 1958 and became pope on June 21, 1963.

## Paul's Papacy

Pope Paul guided the Roman Catholic Church through a tumultuous time in its history. His predecessor, John XXIII, had called an ecumenical council (Vatican Council II, 1962–65) for the purpose of

9

modernizing and redefining the Church, but died in the middle of
it. Paul helped set the stage for Vatican Council II with his October 18, 1962, letter to Amleto Cicognani, secretary of state to Pope
John XXIII, and was elected as a candidate who was thought capable
of keeping the council from spinning out of control while reconciling
conservative and progressive forces within the Church. Paul guided
the council to its completion and made numerous though largely
unpublicized contributions.

Paul mostly succeeded in implementing the council. Although
many priests, religious, and lay persons left the Church in the wake
of the shock, disillusion, miscommunication, and aberrations that accompanied the postconciliar transition, no major schisms occurred,
and the Church came in touch with the modern world. Paul's ability
to preserve the Church's integrity, tradition, and unity amid tumultuous change and conflict is testimony to his skills as a diplomat and
administrator.

One of the most impressive pastoral dimensions of Paul's papacy
was his compassion for Catholics who were unable to live up to
their vows as a priest, nun, or married person. Paul decentralized
the annulment process by granting authority to local marriage tri-
bunals, and simplified the process for laicizing priests and nuns.
He implemented these pastoral policies while affirming the ideals
and responsibilities underlying these vocational commitments and
encouraging individuals to fulfill them.

As Peter Hebblethwaite points out in *Paul VI: The First Modern
Pope*, "Some said that if Pope John's key word was *aggiornamento* [updating], Paul's motto was *avvicinamento* [coming closer to
people]. He had found a new way to address all people of good will."

## Little Known Facts about Paul VI

* He studied for the priesthood from home, became archbishop
  without ever serving as a parish priest, and though not yet a
  cardinal was seriously considered for the papacy in 1958.

* He was known as the Pilgrim Pope because of his extensive travels.
  He broke with the papal precedent of staying inside Italy and
  traveled to Africa, India, the Holy Land, Australia, South America,

Indonesia, Sri Lanka, Hong Kong, the Philippines, and the United States.

◆ Paul's firm but nonconfrontational policy of dialogue and negotiation with the Iron Curtain countries — seeking religious freedom concessions whenever possible — referred to as *Ostpolitik* or East politics, created a foundation from which Pope John Paul II would help bring down Communism in Eastern Europe.

◆ Always sensitive to cultural considerations, in 1966 Paul released Catholics from the obligation of refraining from meat on Fridays (except in Lent) providing that they substitute an appropriate means of fasting and asceticism in recollection of the Lord's death on Good Friday. Sadly, few paid attention beyond his retraction of the prohibition of meat.

◆ Paul helped reduce hostilities during the Vietnam War by bringing the parties to the negotiating table for the Paris Peace Talks in 1968.

◆ In 1970, Paul survived an assassination attempt at the Manila airport by Benjamin Mendoza y Amor, a deranged Bolivian known locally as "the mad painter." Mendoza attacked Paul with a foot-long double-edged knife, but was thwarted by Paul's secretary, Don Pasquale Macchi and Bishop Galvin of Singapore. Like John Paul II, Paul VI immediately forgave his attacker.

## Paul's Times

Pope Paul VI helped shape his and our era. Recall what was going on in the world at the time of his pontificate (1963–78):

◆ Assassinations of President Kennedy, Robert F. Kennedy, Reverend Dr. Martin Luther King Jr., Malcolm X, and former Italian prime minister Aldo Moro.

◆ The expansion of the women's and civil rights movements with the goal of equal rights.

◆ The Vietnam conflict.

◆ Watergate.

◆ The energy crisis.

+ Several Middle Eastern wars and continuous unrest.

+ The heightening of the arms race and oppressive policies of the Soviet Union.

+ China's increased engagement in diplomatic and trade relations with the West.

+ The murder of the Israeli hostages at the 1972 Olympics.

+ The rise of the youth culture highlighted in the media by the soaring popularity of the Beatles that coincided approximately with the death of President Kennedy.

## Paul's Signature Contributions

John Paul II deservedly receives much credit for his innovative teachings in the area of sexuality and married life. His "theology of the body" continues to be the subject of much reflection, application, and study at all levels of the Church. Paul VI has three such trademark contributions, in the areas of communications, evangelization, and human development and spirituality. His teachings span the beginning and end of his pontificate, and are a significant part of his papal charter and legacy.

Paul's first encyclical, *Ecclesiam Suam* ("Paths of the Church," August 6, 1964), is a treatise on the art of dialogue and communications. It deals with both internal and external relations — within the Church and with the world, the sacred and the secular realms. His final pastoral letter, the apostolic exhortation *Evangelii Nuntiandi* ("On Evangelization in the Modern World," December 8, 1975), places dialogue in the context of the primary mission of the Church, that of spreading the good news, and links conversion to evangelization. Communication and conversion must go together in order to avoid ego blockages; selfishness is the enemy of solidarity.

Paul's watershed encyclical *Populorum Progressio* ("On the Development of Peoples," March 26, 1967) not only changed the face and direction of Catholic social teaching, but made a significant contribution to global socio-economic policy considerations. Economists, social activists, and politicians took note of Paul's masterpiece because it was original and articulated in a comprehensible and nonpartisan manner. In 1965, Paul also composed a beautiful reflection on life and its possibilities as part of his last will and testament. This essay is found in the Human Development chapter.

Paul built upon *Populorum Progressio* with *Octogesima Adveniens* ("A Call to Action," May 14, 1971), an apostolic letter that developed the insights of *Populorum Progressio* while recognizing the diversity of cultural situations and the importance of local adaptations.

Paul's second to last apostolic exhortation, *Gaudete in Domino* ("On Christian Joy," May 9, 1975), focused on the spirituality necessary for human fulfillment and development. His last major public address, a prayer offered at the funeral of Paul's old friend Aldo Moro (the former Italian prime minister and then leader of the Christian Democratic Party who was abducted and assassinated by the Red Brigades terrorist group) bewailed the mystery of suffering, which paradoxically constitutes both the greatest obstacle and the impetus to faith, fulfillment, and development. Paul's exhortations, insights, and compassion can help it be the latter for us.

Paul was actively involved in the negotiations to free Aldo Moro from his kidnappers, and even offered to exchange himself for the hostage. His prayer at the funeral Mass for Aldo Moro constitutes a modern psalm, an affirmation of faith and hope amid an outcry of grief and disappointment. Paul's lament consoled and united, if only temporarily, the grief-stricken and divided nation of Italy, just as he had united the Church amid a divisive period. It showcased his ability to balance and articulate the depths of life's joys and sorrows, and to emerge praising God and comforting his people.

Paul's words can inspire us to voice our own grievances and sorrows in a spirit of trust in providence, an attitude that is at the core of potential fulfillment from a Christian standpoint — to unite our sufferings with Christ's and thereby contribute to the salvation of the world through participation in Jesus' redemptive death (cf. Col 1:24).

Though moving and profound, Paul's prayer has always been rather obscure — I have never seen it in print other than in the Vatican's newspaper, *L'Osservatore Romano,* when it reported the event in May 1978. Because it effectively serves as Paul's public goodbye, I have chosen to include it as the final meditation in the book.

## Paul and His Protégé

So much has been communicated about Pope John Paul II that we would be remiss if we did not highlight some of the congruities and contrasts between the two pontiffs. John Paul II practiced Paul's communication and development initiatives through his international trips, criticisms of oppressive capitalist practices and structures, and advocacy for third world nations.

We also observe an interesting parallel in the way both pontiffs dealt with suffering. John Paul wrote a magnificent apostolic letter on it, *Salvici Doloris* ("On the Christian Meaning of Human Suffering," February 11, 1984), and showed how to suffer with dignity through his various illnesses and debilitations, ranging from an assassination attempt to a broken hip suffered during a bathtub mishap to Parkinson's to his final public appearances where his great pain was obvious to all.

Paul VI's approach to suffering was more behind the scenes and subtle. Particularly early in his pontificate he offered insightful and compassionate reflections on suffering to audiences of sick and disabled persons. Paul's final days were much less public than John Paul II's, though his agony, particularly on an emotional and spiritual level, was no less. The chapter on suffering contains some of Paul's most profound and inspirational reflections on the subject.

## Paul VI in Papal Context

The admirable character and legacy of John XXIII and John Paul II is almost universally acknowledged in both religious and secular circles. Their contributions, holiness, and charismatic personalities are well documented. How does Paul VI fit in with them, and in what way do significant differences between them shed light on contemporary circumstances?

A whole book could address this question, but lacking such space we will focus on two points of significant relevance to both the Church and individual readers.

Although it is unpopular and almost heretical to acknowledge any deficiencies, however minor, in the pontificates of John XXIII or John

Paul II, we can appreciate them better if we also recognize their short-comings. In each case it involves Church administration, an area in which Paul VI was significantly more prepared due to his longtime service in the Vatican. Every pope and his administration has strengths and weaknesses. From Peter onward, God has used poor human instruments to guide His Church, a testimony to grace and the ongoing presence of the Spirit.

## *John XXIII*

Just as Paul VI has been misunderstood, so has John XXIII. The popular perception of him as a radical progressive is inaccurate. A savvy Church historian, John was not about to be swept away by every theological, pastoral, or cultural current. His good will, common sense, and receptivity to the Spirit moved him to initiate reform in the Church, but he was not regarded as theologically liberal. He was elected pope because he was perceived as someone who would not initiate great changes and who would not occupy the position as long as Pius XII. The same logic may underlie Benedict XVI's succession of John Paul II.

Toward the end of the pontificate of Pius XII and continuing during John's, the methods and teachings of some of the leading Catholic biblical scholars in Rome were attacked by reactionaries who wished to roll back the openness to biblical studies inaugurated by Pius XII in his landmark encyclical *Divino Afflante Spiritu* ("On Promoting Biblical Studies," September 30, 1943). Max Zerwick and Stanislaw Lyonnet, two prominent professors at the Pontifical Biblical Institute, were relieved of their teaching responsibilities for a year.

The doctrinal arm of the Vatican, then known as "The Holy Office" (during Paul's pontificate renamed "The Sacred Congregation for the Doctrine of the Faith"), issued a warning in 1961 about ideas that questioned "the genuine historical and objective truth of Scripture." No biblical scholar himself, John XXIII did not act swiftly to counter this atmosphere of suspicion and repression.

The precise technical nature of the subject, the conservatism of even kindly disposed church officials still adjusting to the Church's new position on the Bible, and the relative ignorance of the general public about modern biblical studies made scholars an easy mark for detractors wishing to publicly distort their record in order to advance a reactionary agenda.

John's age and illness, and the influence of conservative officials in and surrounding the Curia, could not keep him from drawing the line on a crucial issue. In one of the most important papal interventions at the council (cited approvingly by a Protestant observer as evidence of the need for a pope) he sided with critics of the regressive initial draft of the Vatican II document on the Bible and ordered it to be rewritten by a reconstituted commission.

## Paul and Progress on the Bible

When Paul became pope, such repression and regression came to an end. The aforementioned professors were restored to their teaching responsibilities and a progressive, well-received document on the Bible was published by the Pontifical Biblical Commission. "On the Historical Truth of the Gospels" (April 21, 1964) paved the way for the Vatican II document on the Bible, the Dogmatic Constitution on Divine Revelation (*Dei Verbum*), which after tumultuous debate over a three-year period was passed just prior to the end of the council (on November 18, 1965) with 2,344 yes votes and 6 no votes.

On a related note, one of Paul VI's less publicized initiatives was the creation of the Catholic Biblical Federation in 1969 through the Secretariat for Promoting Christian Unity. Pivotal in its establishment was the coordinating efforts of its president, Augustin Cardinal Bea, former professor at the Pontifical Biblical Institute and among the most prominent and respected Catholic biblical scholars at the time.

The Catholic Biblical Federation focuses on the promotion of the Bible in the Church in the different cultural milieus in which it is encountered and seeks to integrate pastoral, contemplative, and critical perspectives. It has published numerous articles on *lectio divina* (holistic reading and praying of inspired texts, preeminently the Bible) in its journal, *Bulletin Dei Verbum*.

From September 14 to 18, 2005, together with the Pontifical Council for Promoting Christian Unity, the Catholic Biblical Federation held an International Congress at the Vatican in celebration of the fortieth anniversary of the promulgation of *Dei Verbum*. Two of the Church's most learned and influential cardinals, Walter Kasper and Carlo Martini, S.J., presented detailed papers on the evolution and current status of the Bible in the Church, and numerous bishops, educators, and scholars spoke or presented papers. The transcripts and other helpful guidance on the Bible can be found on the Federation's website, c b f.org.

## Paul the Administrator

One of the most overlooked strengths of Paul's pontificate was his administration of the Church. Paul was very good at appointing suitable persons to positions of leadership and responsibility within the Church and did not immediately rein them in when they diverted from his expectations.

For example, he supported Cardinal Suenens's advocacy of the charismatic movement and tolerated his manipulation of the media and occasional criticisms because he recognized his sincerity and loyalty. Paul VI elevated to archbishop and cardinal status the last three popes, so he certainly recognized quality when he saw it.

During the papal transitions of 1978, I remember reading articles speculating on possible successors to Paul and John Paul I. Independently of their unquestioned orthodoxy, what impressed me about the list of *papabili* in 1978 was their dynamism and diversity. So many cardinals from that time, even those too old to be in the running, were prominent for their charisms and contributions to the Church: Suenens, Konig, Baggio, Benelli, Pignedoli, Alfrink, Casaroli, Spellman, Wright, and Villot are just a few that come to mind.

Because Paul did not travel as much as John Paul II, he had more time to attend to the administration of the Church, and his reform of the Curia and willingness to delegate and decentralize resulted in a comparatively competent bureaucracy. Like any pope, Paul inherited and carried a significant amount of "dead wood" in the Vatican, and he was both compassionate and prudent in his cultivation of a more effective organization.

Because of his age and administrative competence, and perhaps as a balance to John Paul II, Benedict seems to be more focused on organizational matters. His voluminous publications during his term as president of the Sacred Congregation for the Doctrine of the Faith attests to his considerable writing and organizational skills.

In summary, Paul was an important component of the blessed papacies of the late twentieth century. He was an intuitive prophet, student of human nature, and competent administrator, a person in touch with the signs and spirit of the times — he devoted practically an entire papal audience, April 16, 1969, to the latter — and a spiritual leader adept at managing the tension between progress and fidelity to tradition. Reflection on his teachings in the concrete circumstances of our lives can help us emulate his balancing tendencies in our polarized world.

## The Sense of the Faithful about Paul

I have dialogued on Paul VI throughout the United States and Europe with theologians, biblical scholars, professors, priests, sisters, and laypersons. A consistent undercurrent in our conversations has been the obscured greatness of Paul VI and the enduring prophetic relevance of his papacy and teachings. Paul's press and public image may have been sub par, but the effects of his words and actions on the Church and world during his fifteen-year pontificate, particularly amid the obstacles and challenges he faced, give rise to a surprising but credible assertion.

With the passage of time and the reevaluation of historians, Paul VI will undergo a rehabilitation and be remembered not only as a mystic and prophet, which he is regarded as now, but as a great pope who arguably had more influence over modern Catholicism than any other pontiff. Paul oversaw more fundamental changes than any other pope and, despite many conflicts and controversies, somehow managed to hold the Church together without repressing the Spirit or the faithful.

## Testimonies to Paul VI

"So that is the way life goes, your eminence, you should really be sitting here now." (Paul VI to Cardinal Lercaro, as Lercaro knelt before Paul in congratulation of his election as pope)

"If Montini were a cardinal, I would have no hesitation in voting for him at the conclave." (Cardinal Roncalli, the future Pope John XXIII, in response to a question put to him at a meeting of academics on the Isola San Giorgio)

"I have neither the 'wisdom of the heart' of Pope John nor the preparation and culture of Pope Paul, but I am in their place."

(Pope John Paul I)

"We wish to pursue with patience but firmness that serene and constructive dialogue that Paul VI had at the base of his plan and program for pastoral action. The principal theme for this was set forth in his great encyclical *Ecclesiam Suam,* namely, that men, as men, should know one another, even those who do not share our faith."

(Pope John Paul I)

"I was constantly amazed at his profound wisdom and his courage and also by his constancy and patience in the difficult post conciliar period of his pontificate. As helmsman of the Church, the bark of Peter, he knew how to preserve a providential tranquility and balance in even the most critical moments, when the Church seemed to be shaken from within, and he always maintained unhesitating hope in the Church's solidity." (Pope John Paul II)

"In the course of his life he was not always understood. He had his cross, bore 'insults' and was 'spat upon. . . .' Love is therefore an act of reparation to his memory." (Pope John Paul II)

The gigantic figure [*la figura gigantesca*] of this great pope taught us — at a difficult period in the life of the church and through a daily martyrdom of worry and work — what it really means to love and serve Christ and souls." (Pope John Paul II)

"Having lived with John Paul II and having listened to him publicly and privately, I must say that you could never get two popes who were as close in their thinking as Paul VI and John Paul II." (Fr. [now Bishop] John Magee, former English-language secretary to both popes)

## Pope Paul on Pope Paul

During his weekly general audience on November 25, 1970, Pope Paul VI offered this eloquent reflection on his papal vocation in relation to Jesus. It reads like a modern confession of faith reminiscent of Peter's at Caesarea Philippi (cf. Mt 16:13–20).

The scene is history, our own history, our own time, today, in which we are looking for "the signs of the times." It is an uneven scene, for it is full of light and darkness and is devastated by the blasts of apparently irresistible hurricanes: modern ideologies. Yet there are also a few spring breezes — the breath of the Spirit, who "blows where he will" (Jn 3:8).

There are three actors on this stage: one, filling it completely, is the incalculable number of the people of today, growing, rising, aware as never before, equipped with formidable tools that give them power that has something prodigious, angelical, diabolical, salutary, and murderous about it. It makes them lords of the earth and sky, and often slaves to themselves.

They are giants, yet they totter weakly and blindly, in agitation and fury, in search of rest and order. They know about everything, and are skeptical about everything and their own destiny. They are unbridled in the flesh and foolish in the mind....

One feature seems to be common to all of them: they are unhappy, something essential is lacking. Who can get near them? Who can instruct them about the things that are necessary for life, when they know so many superfluous things? Who can interpret for them and, through truth, resolve the doubts that are tormenting them? Who can reveal to them the call that they have implicitly in their hearts?

The crowds are an ocean — they are humanity. They hold the stage and are passing slowly but tumultuously across it. It is humankind that makes history....

But there enters another character. He is small, like an ant, weak, unarmed, as tiny as a *quantité négligeable*. He tries to make his way through the throng of peoples; he is trying to say something.

He becomes unyielding and tries to make himself heard; he assumes the appearance of a teacher, a prophet. He assures them that what he is saying does not come from himself, but is a secret and infallible word, a word with a thousand echoes, resounding in the thousand languages of humankind.

But what strikes us most in the comparison we make between the personage and his surroundings is disproportion: in number, in quality, in power, in means, in topicality. ... But that little man — you will have guessed who he is: the apostle, the messenger of the Gospel — is the witness. In this case it is the Pope, daring to pit himself against humankind. David and Goliath? Others will say Don Quixote.... A scene irrelevant, outmoded, embarrassing, dangerous, ridiculous. This is what one hears said, and the appearances seem to justify these comments.

But when he manages to obtain a little silence and attract a listener, the little man speaks in a tone of certainty that is all his own. He utters inconceivable things, mysteries of an invisible world that is yet near us, the divine world, the Christian world, but mysteries....

Some laugh; others say to him: we will hear you another time, as they said to St. Paul in the Areopagus at Athens (Acts 17:32–33).

However, someone there has listened, and always listens, and has perceived that in that plaintive but assured voice there can be distinguished two singular and most sweet accents, which resound wonderfully in the depths of their spirits: one is the accent of truth and the other is the accent of love.

They perceive that the word is the speaker's only in the sense that he is an instrument: it is a Word in its own right, the Word of Another. Where was that Other, and where is He now? He could not and cannot be other than a living Being, a Person who is essentially a Word, a Word made man, the Word of God.

Where was and where is the Word of God made man? For it was and is now clear that he was and is now present! And this is the third actor on the world stage: the actor who stands above it all and fills the whole stage wherever he is welcomed, by a distinct yet not uncustomary way for human knowledge: the way of faith.

O Christ, is it you? You, the Truth? You, Love? Are you here, here with us? In this so much developed, so confused world? This world so corrupt and cruel when it decides to be content with itself, and so innocent and so lovable when it is evangelically childlike?

This world, so intelligent, but so profane, and often deliberately blind and deaf to your signs? This world which you, fountain of love, loved unto death; you, who revealed yourself in love? You, salvation, you the joy of the human race. You are here with the Church, your sacrament and instrument. Does it proclaim you and convey you?

This is the perennial drama that develops over the centuries and that finds in our journey an instant of indescribable reality. Let us spiritually take part in it all together, dearest brethren and children.

*Chapter 2*

# A Personal Word
# about Pope Paul VI

I owe much of my growth as a person and believer to the changes Paul VI instituted within the Catholic Church. I was in grade school when these began taking effect: the lifting of the ban against meat on Fridays, the reform of the Mass and the change from Latin to English, the advent of folk Masses, the loosening of priests' and nuns' dress code, the personalizing of the rite of Confession (including the opportunity to go "face-to-face"), greater openness to the world and other religions, increased interest in social justice, and greater emphasis on the Bible in both the Mass and lay spirituality.

When I went to the University of Michigan, I got involved in a very active Newman Center. I was exposed to Catholic theology, Bible studies, ecumenical activities, Christian fellowship, social justice ministries and activists, and uplifting folk Masses. The priests related to the students on an even, one-to-one level, something that I wasn't used to.

Pope Paul VI died the summer before my sophomore year in college, but by then his progressive mandate for the Church was firmly in place. I began reading some of his encyclicals and gradually accumulated a library of books on the Bible, theology, and spirituality.

When I moved to Boston, I got involved in a student parish that was much like the Newman Center in Ann Arbor. I began taking graduate-level courses in biblical studies, theology, and adult education. Such courses were rarely accessible to laypersons prior to Paul VI's pontificate.

At the age of twenty-three, I began leading a Bible study and receiving spiritual direction (one-on-one discussions with a sister, priest,
or trained layperson about how God was working in my life, and how
I was responding), which I have continued to this day. I enrolled in
a yearlong intensive training program for adult religious educators. It
provided training in psychology, Scripture, and adult education methods from outstanding professors at various Boston universities and
seminaries.

I attended weekend retreats in which I was exposed to such
disciplines as Jungian psychology, logotherapy, centering prayer,
modern theories of adult development, and the spiritual exercises
of St. Ignatius.

I would never have had these opportunities were it not for the
decentralization and resulting liberties Paul set in motion. His progressive writings and teachings encouraged enthusiasm, experimentation,
and adaptation that despite aberrations led to a more relevant faith
and vibrant Church and an informed and involved laity. I rarely came
into contact with clergy, institutions, or parishes that abused the reform process through inappropriate innovations or experimentation,
though quite a few pushed the envelope. In any event it was never
to the point where the core of Catholic teaching and worship (the
Mass) was compromised or affected adversely.

One example of an abuse occurred at the student parish I joined at
Michigan. The pastoral staff replaced masculine language in the Scripture readings with inclusive language before the bishops approved
this. Did it have a negative effect on the liturgy? Probably not, since
at that time inclusive language was "in." However, it was nonethe-
less an inappropriate initiative, particularly since the original language
biblical texts were not consulted and thus in some way the meaning
of the text could have been changed slightly by these insertions. At
a lectors meeting, we were told that if we were uncomfortable with
the changes, we didn't have to lector. Coercion and intransigence
can come from all sides, and each of us is capable of it.

I remember being invited to dinner by a priest who was a theology
professor and to whom I mentioned that I liked Paul VI. He said that
he did too, but he disagreed with Paul VI's position on contraception
and felt great pain over the issue. I recently came across his name in

a book on the subject. This was one of many opportunities I had to enter into dialogue on hot issues within the Church and society.

One of the reasons I resonated with Paul VI was that he took a moderate position on issues, thereby infuriating extremists on both ends of the spectrum. He was under enormous pressure from both radicals and reactionaries, yet somehow he navigated a middle course. Unfortunately, moderates are usually not positioned or passionate enough to drown out or subdue the protests of extremists, and thus Paul VI was widely criticized during the later years of his pontificate and has been largely forgotten or even vilified since. Even high quality biographies of John Paul II generally fail to give Paul VI his due and assess his pontificate in a balanced and informed manner.

Paul VI usually cushioned his teachings with an acknowledgment of their challenging nature and an exhortation to be gentle and compassionate toward ourselves and others when we fall short in our implementation efforts. Paul VI always left room for individuals to exercise discretion and creativity within moral boundaries in order to find the spiritual path appropriate to them.

Conversely, when I read Pope John Paul II, I feel like I am being taught black and white concepts that I am under obligation to accept and practice as instructed, as they are God's will and in my best interests. While I follow and have derived much benefit from his teachings, particularly his theology of the body and his untiring promotion of human dignity and rights, I feel more respect and admiration than closeness, though I am aware of the great affection so many feel for him.

While I felt like I could respectfully and privately disagree with John Paul II on minor points, usually involving particular applications where I am not even sure there was a real disagreement, I don't get the impression that he would have been affected by my perspective. He lived and thought out his teachings so intensely for so long that I think it would have been difficult for him to incorporate alternative perspectives.

When I read Paul VI, I feel the presence of a guide who is journeying alongside me. I believe that he would welcome my feedback and concerns, and encourage me to responsibly and in good conscience adapt his message to my circumstances. As a diplomat, Paul was accustomed to negotiation and dialogue, while John Paul was a professor communicating his knowledge on a complex subject.

I sense that Paul expects something positive from me in accordance with my potential, but when I fall short his words encourage, correct, and console rather than denounce. When I reflect on his life, papacy, and teachings and consider their application to my life, I do so with enthusiasm and hope, free of stifling pressures and debilitating guilt.

I rejoice at the opportunity to expand my horizons through extensive exposure to a modern prophet. I feel blessed to have the opportunity to dialogue with one of the greatest popes and mystics in Church history and a man with an uncommon grasp of the state and challenges of modern life in light of the Christian message. I wrote this book to share this empowering privilege.

## Why I Wrote This Book

I have a passion to share the message and legacy of Paul VI because of his transformational influence in my life and his significant contribution to the Church and the world, which has mostly gone unrecognized.

At the time of the composition of this book, there are a number of books in print in English on Pius XII, John XXIII, and John Paul I, but the only major works on Paul VI are long out of print. Consequently there is a huge information void pertaining to Paul VI, particularly among young Catholics. The perception exists that the only significant events of his pontificate were his administration of Vatican II and the issuance of *Humanae Vitae* and *Populorum Progressio*.

## Paul's Accessible Quality

Complementing my personal, historical, ecclesiastical, and spiritual reasons for writing this book is a practical one, perhaps most important to the reader: Besides being prophetic and profound, Paul VI is comparatively (for a pope) easy to read, providing that you take your time.

Paul's diplomatic and personal sensitivities, cultural refinement, literary skills, and subject knowledge are such that he cultivates his thoughts, measures his words, and offers nuances of insight that will escape us if we proceed in haste. We have to condition ourselves to reread Paul's comments and reflect on them deliberately in order to assimilate them and extract their abundance of meaning and applications.

One does not become a high-ranking diplomat or pope by communicating at a third-grade level, so we have to be prepared for compound sentences, pregnant phrases that invite protracted reflection, and a refined vocabulary. Paul was a natural writer who lived before the dumbing down trends of modern publishing. It would not be a bad idea to have a dictionary nearby for the occasional instances when Paul invites us to expand our vocabulary.

Unlike John Paul II, Paul is literary rather than philosophical by nature and does not belabor points for conceptual or argumentative purposes as one would in an academic or juridical environment. As a diplomat, Paul was primarily concerned with his audience's reception and comprehension of his message.

Paul was well acquainted with the outstanding Catholic novelists and spiritual writers of the twentieth century, and as any good writer will tell you, reading great literature inevitably enhances your writing.

C. S. Lewis counseled practice to those who wished to improve their writing. Paul acquired plenty of practice in drafting documents as Pius XII's pro-secretary of state, so he was already an experienced craftsman by the time he became pope.

Upon hearing that Monsignor Montini (the future Paul VI) had been transferred to the see of Milan, Cardinal Roncalli (the future John XXIII) commented, "Where else will he [Pius XII] find someone capable of writing a letter or drafting a document in the way he can?"

## Prophetic Exemplification

Perhaps the best illustration of the relevance for today of the topics explored in this book is his most famous speech, his October 4, 1965, address to the U.N. General Assembly. It was one of the most important speeches of the twentieth century because it affirmed eloquently, forcefully, and coherently the primacy of peace as a universal modern value.

Current events and recent history reveal the pertinence and tragic rejection of Paul's assertion. With respect to U.S. militarism, scrutiny uncovers a common thread of misleading rationales and associated costs far beyond what is acknowledged by the government and mass media. This applies to both brief and protracted engagements.

## The Message and the Media

Ironically the entertainment media often fills in the gaps left by the news media.

The Vietnam War was justified by the domino theory, but as acknowledged in *The Fog of War*, a 2004 documentary focusing on the perspective of one of its architects, former U.S. Secretary of Defense Robert McNamara, such presuppositions were vastly incorrect.

The invasion of Iraq was justified as preemptive, a rationale that applied en masse would lead all of civilization into conflict. Its prominent attributes — defense contractor controversies, misleading and demagogic disclosures to the public, torture of prisoners and violation of detainee rights, and loss of international credibility and goodwill — are a sad refrain.

Taking as its starting point President Eisenhower's warning about the military industrial complex, a film released in 2005, *Why We Fight,* provides various perspectives on the motives and influences underlying not only the Iraq invasion but other U.S. military engagements and militaristic policies in the post–World War II era.

Even smaller conflicts reek of flagrant violations of international law and human rights. Euphemistically labeled "Operation Just Cause," the 1989 U.S. invasion of Panama was condemned by the U.N. General Assembly and the Organization of American States. The U.S. government and mass media conveniently focused on the drug trafficking and apprehension of the dictator of Panama, General Manuel Noriega, while ignoring unsavory details such as fallout from Panama's eventual control of the canal and rumors of impending nationalization of U.S. business interests in Panama.

An officer who participated in the invasion told me that the "just cause" slogan was widely recognized as a ruse and various uncomplimentary terms were sarcastically appended to it. The 1992 Oscar-winning documentary *The Panama Deception* exposes its shadow side. Another outstanding film, the 1989 Paulist Pictures production *Romero,* concludes with an ominous reference to Reagan administration policies toward El Salvador that accentuated the civil conflict.

A pattern emerges: the U.S. government and corporations choose violence as a means to achieve economic and political ends, the mainstream media compromises its reporting, independent filmmakers produce revealing documentaries, and only a minority of the Christian populace protests or even notices. Highlights of Paul's U.N. speech should be required reading for any Christian seeking to read the signs of the times in today's militaristic and war-ravaged climate.

## The Topical and Personal Relevance of Paul's Plea

While I was selecting excerpts from Paul's speech it became apparent that he touched upon all the topics of this book. As usual, his message was balanced, cohesive, and poignant. In breaking the speech down into manageable portions and reading it anew, I discovered that a personal as well as communal and global challenge was being issued.

When I practice *lectio divina* on the excerpts and consider their application to my life, I experience the issues addressed by Paul as profoundly personal. Actualization of Paul's message, and in particular the values and virtues highlighted in this book, begins with each of us.

Paul's catechetical and evangelical genius is evident in the way he draws us into the subject while conveying in a reassuring manner that he is likewise struggling with the issues. His stock phrase is "whether we [as opposed to *you*] like it or not." Paul's dialogical and self-reflective approach is not imposing or judgmental and therefore can bypass our defenses.

Because John Paul II's language is more philosophical, it can be easier to keep his teachings abstract and remote and project them onto others. We criticize fellow believers' "cafeteria Catholicism / Christianity" (i.e., picking and choosing among doctrines and disciplines) while failing to recognize it in ourselves.

It is tempting to reject John Paul's dignity of life ethics with respect to immigration, war, and related human rights offenses. Pragmatism and nationalism can take precedence over core Catholicism — which is ultimately about love, the one virtue directly identified with God in

the New Testament (cf. 1 Jn 4:8, 16). Paul warns about such ideologies in his U.N. speech, as John Paul II would in his October 2, 1979,
and October 5, 1995, addresses to the U.N. General Assembly.

## The Logic of the Order

The chapters are arranged chronologically according to the events
and publications of Paul's papacy and for continuity. The first topic
is dialogue, the subject of Paul's first encyclical and a term closely
associated with him. The second topic is peace because it was the
theme of Paul's historic trip to New York the next year, 1965.

Chastity follows love because of the inherent connection and the
timing of the related encyclical (*Humanae Vitae,* July 25, 1968), with
human development next because of the chronological proximity
of its encyclical (*Populorum Progressio,* March 26, 1967). Joy and
evangelization are the concluding topics because they are the final
apostolic exhortations that Paul wrote, and spiritually and pastorally
they bring his papacy full circle.

The number of excerpts in each chapter is based on the amount of
material available and my subjective assessment of its contemporary
relevance and historical importance. However, chapter length alone
is insufficient indication of the quality of the material. For example,
the chapters on dialogue, peace, and evangelization are of average
length although Paul's contributions in these areas are as significant
as in the areas of longer chapters such as chastity, joy (spirituality),
and human development. Paul could say a lot with a little, and he
spoke volumes with his actions, particularly with respect to the three
former topics.

In each chapter I introduce the subject by weaving in relevant
facts, insights, observations, and anecdotes related to Paul's character, teaching, and papacy. I place Paul's thoughts in their personal,
historical, and contemporary context. We get to know Paul the person and pope concurrent with Paul the mystic, teacher, and fellow
disciple.

*Chapter 3*

# A Short Course in
# *Lectio Divina*

In an address to the Catholic Biblical Federation International Congress on September 16, 2005, Pope Benedict XVI offered the most enthusiastic and progressive promotion of the practice of *lectio divina* by any modern pontiff. He said, "I would like in particular to recall and recommend the ancient tradition of *lectio divina*... If it is effectively promoted, this practice will bring to the Church — I am convinced of it — a new spiritual springtime. As a strong point of biblical ministry, *lectio divina* should therefore be increasingly encouraged, also through the use of new methods, carefully thought through and in step with the times."

*Lectio divina* is the Church's oldest and official model for prayerfully reading Scripture, and is particularly appropriate to Paul's teachings because they are biblically based and correspondingly contain multiple applications. As indicated in Pope Benedict's remarks it is also a tool of the times (cf. Mt 16:3) in the sense of being suited to the needs of contemporary believers and intellectual, scientific, and spiritual development.

## *Applying* Lectio Divina *to Paul VI's Meditations*

Paul VI's meditations are the fruit of his *lectio divina* on the Bible, the teachings of the Church, and life. Thus they are eminently suitable for our own *lectio divina,* particularly given Paul's articulate and precise manner and his charism and authority as pope. We are better able to assimilate the wisdom, energy, and depth of Paul's message when we engage it holistically through *lectio divina*. In the conclusions to

each topic I have give additional help and guidance for the use of
*lectio divina* with Pope Paul's texts.

## Divine Reading

You can take a number of approaches to these meditations. You can
browse, read, study, pray, or meditate upon them. Each approach is
beneficial and suitable to various purposes. There is obviously some
overlap. *Lectio divina,* Latin for divine reading, is the ancient model
that integrates these in a holistic and transformational manner.

*Lectio divina* is based on ancient Hebrew principles of biblical
interpretation and prayer that evolved during the transition from an
oral / aural to a written culture. It is a fluid, interactive synthesis of:

1. reading/listening (when the source of inspiration or instruction
   is words) or sensing/observing (when the source is nature or a
   life experience)

2. meditation (repeating a word or affirming an experience and
   applying it to our life)

3. prayer (active dialogue with God; communicating our feelings
   and response to God's word and our life situation)

4. contemplation (the receptive dimension of dialogue with God;
   quiet, simple presence before the Lord)

5. action (living the word or message we have received)

In practicing *lectio divina,* we are engaging both Catholic and
catholic (universal) concepts and activities that can bring us closer
as brothers and sisters. The essential elements of *lectio divina* are
fundamental to most religions and spiritualities, and are generically
human. As part of practicing their spirituality, people naturally experience these activities and go through at least some part of this process
even if they are unfamiliar with its terminology and structure.

### Practicing Lectio Divina

*Lectio divina* is not speed reading. We relax and take our time. We
step back from the frantic pursuit of personal agendas and precise
objectives. *Lectio divina* is meant to put us in touch not with narrow
conceptions of success, but with God's Spirit and our true selves

and, by relation, others and a fuller experience of nature, life, and Christian discipleship.

We read until we find something that strikes or touches us. Sometimes we find this within one passage in the Bible or in our case one excerpt from Paul's teachings; other times we may need to go through several. Much depends on our mood, life situation, practical circumstances (e.g., the time and space we have), and reading style and objectives.

The Ancient Near Eastern concept of word (in Hebrew, *davar*) and the classical concept (in Greek, *logos*) were much more dynamic than our present Western concept. It was an energy, force, reason, or emotion that evoked an action or response. A word had power to affect reality. We observe how words can break down or build up.

This portion of text, or the experience, emotion, image, or memory it evokes, can console, enlighten, or challenge us. Sometimes things come to our attention that make us uncomfortable. Perhaps we are out of kilter in an area of our lives and need stimuli to jolt us to our senses. We may be feeling down and discouraged and need something to regenerate and reorient us.

Ultimately, we have to trust that God will provide a word or stimulus to help us get through the day in a peaceful and holy manner. *Lectio divina* is a course in "letting go and letting God" in a responsible fashion. Twelve-step spirituality adherents know this challenge well. We do our part by opening ourselves to God's initiative. We surrender to Someone greater rather than seek to impose ourselves or our agenda on God, others, and life. This compliant, counter-cultural, receptivity is essential to our holistic development and fulfillment.

Once we find our word, thought, image, insight, or prayer for the day, we let it become part of us, a centering point to return to during the day. If it is something written or verbal, we repetitively recite it slowly and aloud (if not disturbing to others) and allow it to percolate in our hearts. Gradually it moves into the depths of our being and subconscious, even though we may not sense this. We should not be discouraged by dryness or apparent lack of insights or emotional or sensate stimulations. Efforts are our business, results are God's.

## Lectio Divina *Up Close and Personal*

Most times that I practice *lectio divina* I do not feel particularly inspired. I don't have an angel whispering in my ear directing me to
repeat a specific word or phrase. I just go with what comes closest
to touching me and being relevant. I proceed with my *lectio divina*
according to my capacities and the movement of the Spirit within me.

I am not concerned with practicing *lectio divina*"right," but sincerely. I don't have to conform rigidly to the guidelines in this book,
as if they came from the handbook of a master. I do what comes
naturally, what I have the energy and inclination for, what the Spirit
seems to be urging within me, while keeping in mind the general
procedures. *Lectio divina* follows the pattern of a relationship in that
each person and encounter is unique, and since God is the controlling party, there is no discernible script. The more relaxed, pliable,
and sincere I am, the better I will fare, even if I don't necessarily feel
uplifted.

Some days, particularly when I am down and hopefully humble,
I feel a sense of greater openness to Scripture even before I begin
reading. I anticipate receiving a message because my heart is open
and I feel less distracted.

My greatest inspirations usually come when I am going through a
difficult time and need a spiritual bolster. I am more disposed to intuit
and accept the challenging, suffering-related message of the Bible
when I am already living it. Suffering can strip us of superficialities
and distractions and focus us on what is essential. Lament-rich books
such as the Psalms, Job, and Jeremiah can be cathartic and consoling
*lectio divina* material when we are struggling and need a spiritual and
emotional release.

## *Making Associations*

In the process of engaging the word of our present *lectio divina,*
we may spontaneously begin recalling other words (an inspirational
passage from the Bible or another spiritual book, a personal insight,
experience, or memory, an element of nature, etc.) as a way of making associations and personal applications. Monks from the Middle
Ages referred to this as "reminiscence."

Reminiscence is not an excuse for following every thought, impulse, or memory and forgetting about the main message we have received. While it is necessary to be flexible and open to the promptings of the Spirit, it is also important to keep our present *lectio divina* word in mind as a radius or point of return. We don't want to reflexively abandon our present inspiration just because other thoughts and associations come to mind.

The ideal is to integrate them in a way that grounds us in the present while incorporating past experiences and insights. This gentle, natural oscillation (both between the stages and activities of *lectio divina* and between the various stimuli that come to our attention) and balancing is in keeping with the rhythmic flow of *lectio divina*.

The purpose of *lectio divina* is not to plow through reading, meditation, prayer, contemplation, and action in a rigidly linear, mechanical manner, but rather to flow with the Spirit and our natural gifts and inclinations. We deepen and personalize our *lectio divina* experience by integrating substantive memories, feelings, and insights that arise with the particular word of the day. *Lectio divina* thereby becomes an integral part of life rather than an isolated experience.

## The Word

The word that touches us can be a phrase, word, or image found directly in the text, or an experience or spiritual movement occasioned by our reflection and prayer. We consecrate (spiritually offer) that word, image, energy, memory, experience, emotion, or insight to God through repetition, application to our life, and, if so moved, reminiscence as part of the meditation stage. We communicate our response to the word we have received and anything else we wish to share (prayer) and listen for His response, receptively resting in His presence (contemplation). And then we try to live the word or message (action).

We "cool down" from the previous stages in contemplation by sitting still and remaining silent, even when a thousand thoughts go through our minds and we squirm in anticipation of the next activity on our agenda. Just being with God, as with a loved one, creates a positive energy that will inevitably overflow into our relationship with ourselves, others, and the natural and material world.

*Lectio divina* is not a spiritually greedy, manipulative method. The intent is less to get something out of the text than to offer ourselves to God through it. If we are granted an insight or an explicit feeling of God's presence, we are grateful, but there is more. Our main purpose is to become more receptive and responsive to God, our true self, and our brothers and sisters. Without a prayerful foundation, our attempts to serve God and others will inevitably become depleted or misdirected. How easy it is for ego, agendas, and life's stressors to intrude.

Life exists through God's word. Nothing comes into being apart from God (cf. Jn 1:3). Accordingly we can practice *lectio divina* not only on the written word of God and derivative forms such as the teachings of the magisterium and the saints, but on any stimuli through which we perceive God is taking the initiative in our life. Examples include an aspect of nature that speaks to us, a significant relationship, experience, or entry in our personal journal, a sacramental encounter (e.g., at Mass, Confession, a wedding, or the Anointing of the Sick), and classic spiritual literature.

We should not exclude God from any aspect of our life. The Word became flesh, and made His dwelling among us (cf. Jn 1:14). Nothing human is beyond His healing and transformational power.

## Praying under Pressure

Most of us have busy lives that periodically or even chronically sidetrack us from life's essentials, our treasures and priorities. Our schedules can get so hectic and cluttered, sometimes through little fault of our own, that the best we can do is spend a few moments with God. Life is full of limitations. It is our attitude, intent, and response that matters.

*Lectio divina* is well suited to this reality. It offers a healthy sanctuary from competition and rigid expectations. It can be adapted to our schedule and capacities. Ideally, we will have fifteen to thirty minutes for reflection, but that is not always feasible. The words of Paul VI are likewise amenable to tight schedules because he says a lot with a little, enabling us to make even brief comments reflection fodder for the rest of the day.

Three minutes of meditation on one line of text can make a difference. We allocate the time available and accept what we are able to give to God, provided that we are not being sloppy, lazy, or distracted (e.g., overindulgence in passive pastimes such as video games, spectator sports, television viewing, or Internet surfing). God is capable of providing nourishment for our soul and the world amid our sincere but imperfect efforts. If He desires more from us, He'll let us know and provide a way for us to comply. Then it's up to us.

## Relax

When I practice *lectio divina,* I put no pressure on myself. I let go and put myself in the hands of God, giving him my warts, wounds, and "whys?" as well as my praise and thanksgiving. The Spirit becomes my mouthpiece, rhythm, and energy.

When a child comes to me, I don't want that child to be anything but relaxed and confident of being accepted. Analogously, our Father's welcome and responsiveness infinitely surpasses ours.

In *lectio divina,* I talk to God and listen to Him. Like the majority of folks, I have difficulty sitting still and slowing down. Either my mind races in every direction or I fall asleep. Success is not how I feel during *lectio divina,* but whether I give myself to God as best I can, as spouses offer themselves to their partners. The most frequent image in the Bible for God's relationship with His people is that of marriage (cf. Is 54:5; Jer 3:20; Hos 1–3; Eph 5:21–33).

***Lectio Divina* Consequences**    Positive feelings and results are a desirable byproduct of *lectio divina,* but they are not my criteria of success. Fidelity to God's will is, however difficult this may be. I desire spiritual peace and joy, which is not the same as pleasure or bliss. I expect and allow God to console me in His own time and way. I let myself be comforted by His presence and word, however contrary it may be to my expectations. I then resolve to put the word into action. The ultimate criterion of the efficacy of my *lectio divina* experience is its effect on my life, the fruits I bear in word and deed.

## Building Bridges

The "word" or message I receive during my *lectio divina* becomes a bridge to my day, a still and centering point of spiritual refuge and refocusing. It can also provide emotional and physical benefits by slowing me down and helping me regain perspective and rhythm. Unfortunately, it usually isn't long before I forget this word and transgress it due to some combination of chaotic activity, over-stimulation, selfishness, ignorance, immaturity, or weakness in the face of temptation.

However, if I really want this word to become a bridge and beacon to my day, I can recall it, ask the Spirit to work on my heart, pick myself up and try again (cf. Prov 24:16), and let God's affirming gaze bring me to my senses (cf. Lk 15:17; 22:61). My fragility and sinfulness reminds me to let go of my propensity to judge others. There are more fruitful outlets for my energies.

## Paul's Literary and Oratory Style

Paul VI employed a broad but accessible vocabulary and did not simplify or generalize concepts in deference to popular culture. He had a way of bringing spirituality down to earth while invoking both common sense and fresh intellectual insights. As he observed in his June 16, 1971, audience, what a marvelous and moral thing it is to "think well," to reason things out prayerfully rather than bow to society's pressures and conditioning.

Paul's personal library of over six thousand volumes is reflected in the abundant references (particularly to Saints Paul, Augustine, and Thomas Aquinas) that accompany his communications. One of Paul's first requests upon becoming pope was "please send me my books." A large freight car was required.

A former teacher, Father Persico, observed: "He was very fine, with surprising gifts as a writer and an eloquence based on facts and ideas and was absolutely anti-rhetorical. . . . He would have made his reputation as a famous journalist had he not chosen another way of life." Paul once told his confidant Jean Guitton that being pope was rather like being a writer. His papacy was a letter to the Church and the world about the richness and challenge of the Gospel.

## The Utility of Daily Meditations

Daily meditations are becoming a necessity in our increasingly chaotic and secularized world. Most people don't have time to read treatises. Some reading and reflection time is necessary each day in order to maintain our bearings. Social, psychological, technological, and physiological pursuits can work hand in hand with spirituality, but they should not displace it. Pope Paul VI would tell us to appreciate and utilize what human disciplines and culture have to offer without neglecting or compromising our conscience and spiritual activities.

## Length and Flow of the Meditations

Pope Paul's teachings are presented chronologically within each topic. This enables us to see both the consistency and development of his thought, the way he adapted it to new circumstances without compromising its essence.

The lengths of the meditations depend on their message. Some of Paul's thoughts are pithy and stand alone, while others bear his extended explanation. If a given passage is too long or intense for immediate assimilation, break it down and reflect on part of it.

## Selection and Presentation Criteria

I have selected messages that are catholic (universal) as well as Catholic. Most are explicitly Christian, but some are generically spiritual or developmental and constitute a bridge to persons of other faiths. I tried to balance fidelity to Paul's thought with sensitivity to this book's diverse audience. True dialogue does not impose itself on others, but neither does it water down or manipulate its message.

The selections reflect my bias as to what is accessible, relevant, inspiring, and instructive. Process what is helpful and let go of the rest. If a given meditation doesn't speak to you, go to another one. It would be difficult to find a devotional book with which you would resonate completely. Paul and I are up for dialogue, which includes respectful disagreement and accommodation.

## Note on Literary Devices and Exclusive Language

In accordance with papal practice, Pope Paul VI often refers to himself as "we." His successors have dropped this "royal we."

When Paul VI uses masculine terms it is usually apparent from the context when he means both sexes, which is the vast majority of cases, and when he means males exclusively. He means no offense to women, just as he does not purport to call adults adolescents when he refers to his audience as children.

Pope Paul was born in late nineteenth-century Italy and was in his seventies when inclusive language was introduced. Italian women traditionally have not been at the forefront of the feminist movement. As the saying goes, Italian women have no need to strive for equality, for as wives and mothers they already feel superior.

While language is important, attitudes and actions speak loudest. I can use politically correct language while I act condescendingly or deceptively toward the subject of my sensitivity, just as I can use traditional terms while treating the affected person or group with dignity and affection.

We all reflect our times and culture. By understanding Paul's milieu, we can empathetically make adjustments for language and gestures that many in society no longer consider proper.

The meditation headings use inclusive language when referring to both sexes, while retaining the masculine pronoun in reference to God. I appreciate readers' forbearance on these sensitive questions.

## Lectio Divina *in a Group Setting*

Adapting *lectio divina* to a group setting, I once led a Bible study group through Paul's apostolic exhortation on evangelization. Images, phrases, and related experiences stood out for individuals just as in reading the Bible — not surprising given the biblical foundations of *Evangelii Nuntiandi*. The cohesive and inspirational quality of the document was apparent. It was a formation course in evangelization free of condescending or coercive proselytizing.

One of the group members, a retired engineer named O'Leary, was resistant to the *lectio divina* model until faced with an unexpected evangelical and ecumenical opportunity. When he was jailed along with members of local Protestant churches for nonviolent protests at an abortion clinic, the Spirit moved him to suggest that they pray the Our Father together. Since *lectio divina* is a prayerful way of reading, listening, sensing, and living, it is not surprising that a Christian community of diverse perspectives could unite through *lectio divina* of the Our Father.

In an apt commentary on Paul's spiritual legacy, Yves Congar, esteemed French ecclesiologist who helped lay the theological groundwork for Vatican II (and who, like many other pioneers of the council had previously come under suspicion for what later would be recognized as sound teaching), offered this commentary on Paul's death, immediately preceding which he had been praying the Lord's Prayer: "Paul died with the words 'Our Father who art in heaven' on his lips. It was the death he had always prayed for. 'What is the greatest misfortune here below?' he had asked, and answered, 'to be unable to say "Our Father"'" (April 16, 1965). "'What is the Church doing in this world?' he asked on another occasion, and replied, 'Making it possible for us to say "Our Father"'" (March 23, 1966).

# Chapter 4

# The Art of Dialogue

*You give sanction to the great principle that the relations between peoples should be regulated by reason, by justice, by law, by negotiation; not by force, not by violence, not by war, not by fear or by deceit....*

*Peace, as you know, is not built up only by means of politics, by the balance of forces and of interests. It is constructed with the mind, with ideas, with works of peace.*

—Pope Paul VI, Address to the
U.N. General Assembly, October 4, 1965

It has often been observed that Pope Paul VI could not have started Vatican Council II and John XXIII could not have ended it. Paul's cautious nature and keen awareness of the tensions and polarities a council would expose and even exacerbate would likely have kept him from undertaking the daring initiative of John XXIII. Conversely, although a diplomat himself, John would likely have had great difficulty reconciling the conservative and progressive forces sufficiently to compile documents acceptable to all parties. Paul could do this because he was master not only of the art of dialogue but that of compromise as well — a characteristic that would bring him considerable criticism during his papacy.

Paul's first encyclical, *Ecclesiam Suam* ("Paths of the Church," June 6, 1964), contained his analysis of the attitudes and actions necessary for individual Catholics and the Church to interact effectively with the modern world. Its fundamental value was dialogue, a commitment to respectful and hopefully reciprocal communications. Paul exemplified this message throughout his life and papacy, and thus this encyclical stands as a personal testament and key to understanding the way and direction in which he led the Church.

All the major achievements of Paul's papacy contain the mark of dialogue: his ecumenical overtures, particularly to the Eastern Orthodox Church, his eloquent speech at the United Nations, his pivotal participation in negotiations to end the Vietnam War, his landmark social justice writings, *Populorum Progressio* ("On the Development of Peoples," March 26, 1967) and *Octogesima Adveniens* ("A Call to Action," May 14, 1971), his masterpiece on evangelization, *Evangelii Nuntiandi* ("On Evangelization in the Modern World," December 8, 1975) that John Paul II wisely chose to reference and build upon rather than supercede, and perhaps most of all his implementation of the council. He trusted providence and the people (sometimes too much so) and allowed the Spirit to operate within the Church even when human weakness and agendas served as obstacles to and distortions of the council fathers' intentions.

Consequently the Church experienced an unprecedented spiritual, pastoral, and intellectual renewal in the three decades following Vatican II. Only the recentralization and ideological retrenchment that set in during the last decade of John Paul II's pontificate served to retard the enthusiasm and momentum facilitated by Paul VI and other implementers of the council's teachings and initiatives.

This is history, but how is it related to my story?

First, differences between individuals and groups can be negotiated and resolved effectively only by dialogue. The extremes of aggression/oppression and passivity (apathy, indifference) exacerbate divisions and retard communications and cooperation. In my primary relationships and everyday actions, do I exhibit a dialogical, receptive attitude that encourages truthful, heartfelt communications and harmonious, mutually beneficial interactions?

Second, do I support the adoption of dialogical attitudes and interactions on a social, economic, and political scale? Dialogue is communal as well as interpersonal. Do I support politicians who listen and seek the common good (however scarce this breed may be) and oppose those of the "might makes right" mentality? Do I try to build bridges and facilitate reconciliation or do I simply mind my own business and turn the other way when conflicts arise?

Third, am I willing to persevere in dialogue even when it is unsuccessful at first and evokes resistance and even persecution?

Am I willing to follow in Paul VI's footsteps and continue to believe in the power of goodwill and communication even when I find myself in a distinct minority?

Am I willing to accept the consequences of making myself vulnerable to others out of respect for their dignity and free will, rejecting coercive and manipulative tactics and thereby encouraging my counterparts to act according to their highest values?

Like Paul, am I willing to seek common ground and consider alternative viewpoints even from those whose actions and positions are distasteful to me? I don't have to be a diplomat, negotiator, or mediator to be a proponent and model of dialogue. Like charity, dialogue begins at home, with those whom it is often most difficult to understand and reconcile with. Paul's exhortations and insights will provide guidance and inspiration for choosing conciliation and cooperation rather than coercion and conflict.

If I had to pick one characteristic of Paul to take with me each day, it would be the disposition to dialogue. Amid a myriad of communication breakdowns occurring all around me, I can reflect on his guidelines for opening and solidifying communication channels and building bridges.

Following Paul's example, we will start by listening. Persons who met Paul VI as well as John Paul II often commented on their attentiveness and the intense presence and focus that they communicated. At that moment, nothing else seemed to exist for them but the person and encounter before them.

Cardinal Martini, a confidant of Paul selected by him to give one of the Vatican's annual Lenten retreats, remembers him in this way: "Paul VI had a marked capacity for friendship, a surprising respect for whomever spoke to him, a rare ability to show that two were needed in a dialogue, not just one. He made one feel, truly and unpretentiously, that whomever he was speaking to was important to him and from that person he mysteriously expected something decisive. He was ready to give very generously but without ever making his giving a burden. Indeed he seemed to be excusing himself for it, asking that it be seen as something obvious, so that the real, personal aspect of the relationship might not change.

"For this reason he did not see dialogue merely as an instrument but as a method reflecting the dialogical makeup of his personality. And so, without being compelled to say so, he felt close to modern people, close also to those who were distant or who opposed him in theory or in practice. This is why his pontificate, moving rapidly forward in the way prophetically indicated by Pope John XXIII, was to provide for the Church an audience and a worldwide respect in which the charism of mass encounters with people, characteristic of Pope John Paul II, could be freely prepared. . . .

"As the passing of time moves us further and further from the earthly existence of Paul VI, his spiritual figure comes closer to us. More and more we understand that he was truly one of us, a man of our age who freed us from the danger of shutting ourselves up in our age, who helped us dialogue with the past, who gave us the courage and the joy to become contemporaries of Christ."*

Perhaps Paul's closest lay confidant, Jean Guitton, one of the leading Catholic intellectuals of the 1950s and 1960s, wrote a book in which he projected a dialogue with Paul on important issues of modern life and spirituality. After reviewing the manuscript, Paul confirmed that it accurately portrayed his perspective. The book was entitled *The Pope Speaks: Dialogues of Paul VI with Jean Guitton.*

Dialogue became so quickly associated with Paul VI that Simon & Schuster published a book of that name in 1964. Subtitled *Reflections on God and Man* and part of the Credo Perspectives series, it contained excerpts from Paul's teachings selected by Monsignor John G. Clancy.

In this present book we can take up where Guitton left off by imaginatively conversing with Paul through reflection on his words, legacy, and example. We can even develop our own book by writing in the margins of this one or in a separate notebook or journal. The son of a newspaper publisher and himself a voracious reader who extensively annotated his own library, Paul would be proud.

---

*Cardinal Carlo Maria Martini, *Journeying with the Lord* (Staten Island, N.Y.: Alba House, 1987); reprinted with permission.

## DIALOGUE

**Drawing Near to the World through Dialogue** Did not our predecessors, especially Pope Pius XI and Pope Pius XII, leave us a magnificently rich patrimony of teaching which was conceived in the loving and enlightened attempt to join divine to human wisdom, not considered in the abstract, but rather expressed in the concrete language of modern man? And what is this apostolic endeavor if not a dialogue? And did not John XXIII, our immediate predecessor of venerable memory, place an even sharper emphasis on its teaching in the sense of approaching as close as possible to the experience and the understanding of the contemporary world?

And was not the council itself assigned — and justly so — a pastoral function which would be completely focused on the injection of the Christian message into the stream of the thought, of the speech, of the culture, of the customs, of the strivings of man as he lives today and acts in this life?

Even before converting the world, nay, in order to convert it, we must meet the world and talk to it.      —*Ecclesiam Suam,* 1964

**In but Not of the World** In the pursuit of spiritual and moral perfection the Church receives an exterior stimulus from the conditions in which she lives. She cannot remain unaffected by or indifferent to the changes that take place in the world around.

This world exerts its influence on the Church in a thousand ways and places conditions on her daily conduct. The Church, as everyone knows, is not separated from the world, but lives in it.

Hence, the members of the Church are subject to its influence; they breathe its culture, accept its laws and absorb its customs. This imminent contact of the Church with temporal society continually creates for her problematic situations which today have become extremely difficult. On the one hand Christian life, as defended and promoted by the Church, must always take great care lest it should be deceived, profaned or stifled as it must strive to render itself immune from the contagion of error and of evil.

On the other hand, Christian life should not only be adapted to the forms of thought and custom which the temporal environment offers and imposes on her, provided they are compatible with the basic exigencies of her religious and moral program, but it should also try to draw close to them, to purify them, to ennoble them, to vivify and to sanctify them. This task demands of the Church a perennial examination of her moral vigilance, which our times demand with particular urgency and exceptional seriousness....

The great principle enunciated by Christ presents itself again both in its actuality and in its difficulty: To be in the world, and not of the world. It is good for us even today to offer up that highest and most opportune prayer of Christ "who always lives and intercedes for us" (Heb 7:25): "I am not asking that thou shouldst take them out of the world, but that thou shouldst keep them clear of what is evil" (Jn 17:15).     *Ecclesiam Suam,* 1964

**Accepting the Church's Flaws**   We must serve the Church and love her as she is, with a clear understanding of history, and humbly searching for the will of God who assists and guides her even when at times He permits human weakness to eclipse the purity of her features and the beauty of her action. It is this purity and beauty which we are endeavoring to discover and promote.                    —*Ecclesiam Suam,* 1964

**Losing the Sacred in the Secular**   Conformity appears to many as an inescapable and wise course. Those who are not well rooted in Faith and in the observance of Ecclesiastical Law easily think that the time has come for concessions to be made to secular norms of life, as if these were better and as if the Christian can and must make them his own.

This phenomenon of adaptation is noticeable in the philosophical field (how much fashion counts even in the world of thought, which ought to be autonomous and free and only avid and docile before truth and the authority of approved masters!), as well as in the practical field, where it is becoming more and more uncertain and difficult to point out the line of moral rectitude and right conduct....

However it is not our intention to say that perfection consists in remaining changeless as regards external forms which the Church through many centuries has assumed. Nor does it consist in being stubbornly opposed to those new forms and habits which are commonly regarded as acceptable and suited to the character of our times.          —*Ecclesiam Suam,* 1964

**Distinct from the World but Not Indifferent**   See how St. Paul himself formed the Christians of the primitive church: "You must not consent to be yokefellows with unbelievers. What has innocence to do with lawlessness? What is there in common between light and darkness? How can a believer throw in his lot with an infidel?" (2 Cor 6:14–15).

Christian education will always have to remind the student today of his privileged position and of his resultant duty to live in the world but not in the way of the world, according to the above-mentioned prayer of Jesus for His disciples: "I am not asking that thou shouldst take them out of the world, but that thou shouldst keep them clear of what is evil. They do not belong to the world, as I, too, do not belong to the world" (Jn 17:15–16). And the Church adopts this prayer as its own.
                                        —*Ecclesiam Suam,* 1964

**Making Distinctions for Unity**   When the Church distinguishes itself from human nature, it does not oppose itself to human nature, but rather unites itself to it. Just as the doctor who, realizing the danger inherent in a contagious disease, not only tries to protect himself and others from such infection, but also dedicates himself to curing those who have been stricken, so too the Church does not make an exclusive privilege of the mercy which the divine goodness has shown it, nor does it distort its own good fortune into a reason for disinterest in those who have not shared it. Rather in its own salvation it finds an argument for interest in and for love for anyone who is either close to it and can at least be approached through universal effort to share its blessings.          —*Ecclesiam Suam,* 1964

**The Transcendent Origins of Dialogue**   See, then, Venerable Brethren, the transcendent origin of the dialogue. It is found in the very plan of God. Religion, of its very nature, is a relationship between God and man. Prayer expresses such a relationship in dialogue. Revelation, i.e., the supernatural relationship which God Himself, on His own initiative, has established with the human race, can be represented as a dialogue in which the Word of God is expressed in the Incarnation and therefore in the Gospel.                                           —*Ecclesiam Suam,* 1964

**A Divine Invitation to Love**   The fatherly and holy conversation between God and man, interrupted by original sin, has been marvelously resumed in the course of history. The history of salvation narrates exactly this long and changing dialogue which begins with God and brings to man a many-splendored conversation.

It is in this conversation of Christ among men (cf. Bar 3:38) that God allows us to understand something of Himself, the mystery of His life, unique in its essence, trinitarian in its persons; and He tells us finally how He wishes to be known; He is Love; and how He wishes to be honored and served by us: Love is our supreme commandment....

The dialogue of salvation began with charity, with the divine goodness: "God so loved the world as to give His only-begotten Son" (Jn 3:16); nothing but fervent and unselfish love should motivate our dialogue.                          —*Ecclesiam Suam,* 1964

**The Freedom of the Dialogue**   The dialogue of salvation did not physically force anyone to accept it; it was a tremendous appeal of love which, although placing a vast responsibility on those toward whom it was directed (cf. Mt 11:21), nevertheless left them free to respond to it or to reject it. Even the number of miracles (cf. Mt 12:38ff.) and their demonstrative power (cf. Mt 13:13ff.) were adapted to the spiritual needs and dispositions of the recipients, in order that their free consent to the divine revelation might be facilitated, without, however, their losing the merit involved in such a consent.        —*Ecclesiam Suam,* 1964

**The Universality of the Dialogue**    The dialogue of salvation was made accessible to all; it was destined for all without distinction (cf. Col 3:11); in like manner our own dialogue should be potentially universal, i.e., all-embracing and capable of including all, excepting only one who would either absolutely reject it or insincerely pretend to accept it.          —*Ecclesiam Suam,* 1964

**The Patient Opportunism of the Dialogue**    The dialogue of salvation normally experienced a gradual development, successive advances, humble beginnings before complete success (cf. Mt 13:31). Ours, too, will take cognizance of the slowness of psychological and historical maturation and of the need to wait for the hour when God may make our dialogue effective. Not for this reason will our dialogue postpone till tomorrow what it can accomplish today; it ought to be eager for the opportune moment; it ought to sense the preciousness of time (cf. Eph 4:16). Today, i.e., every day, our dialogue should begin again; we, rather than those toward whom it is directed, should take the initiative.
—*Ecclesiam Suam,* 1964

**Adapting the Dialogue to the Person**    But it seems to us that the relationship of the Church to the world, without precluding other legitimate forms of expression, can be represented better in a dialogue, not, of course, a dialogue in a univocal sense, but rather a dialogue adapted to the nature of the interlocutor and to factual circumstances (the dialogue with a child differs from that with an adult; that with a believer from that with an unbeliever).

**The Good Faith Nature of the Dialogue**    This type of relationship indicates a proposal of courteous esteem, of understanding and of goodness on the part of the one who inaugurates the dialogue; it excludes the a priori condemnation, the offensive and time-worn polemic and emptiness of useless conversation. If this approach does not aim at effecting the immediate conversion of the interlocutor, inasmuch as it respects both his dignity and his freedom, nevertheless it does aim at helping him and tries to dispose him for a fuller sharing of sentiments and convictions. —*Ecclesiam Suam*, 1964

**The Saving Impulse to Dialogue** Hence, the dialogue supposes that we possess a state of mind which we intend to communicate to others and to foster in all our neighbors: It is a state of mind of one who feels within himself the burden of the apostolic mandate, of one who realizes that he can no longer separate his own salvation from the endeavor to save others, of one who strives constantly to put the message of which he is custodian into the mainstream of human discourse. —*Ecclesiam Suam*, 1964

**Characteristics of Spiritual Communications** The dialogue is, then, a method of accomplishing the apostolic mission. It is an example of the art of spiritual communication. Its characteristics are the following:

1. Clearness above all; the dialogue supposes and demands comprehensibility. It is an outpouring of thought; it is an invitation to the exercise of the highest powers which man possesses. This very claim would be enough to classify the dialogue among the best manifestations of human activity and culture. This fundamental requirement is enough to enlist our apostolic care to review every angle of our language to guarantee that it be understandable, acceptable, and well-chosen.

2. A second characteristic of the dialogue is its meekness, the virtue which Christ sets before us to be learned from Him: "Learn of me, because I am meek and humble of heart" (Mt 11:29). The dialogue is not proud, it is not bitter, it is not offensive. Its authority is intrinsic to the truth it explains, to the charity it communicates, to the example it proposes; it is not a command, it is not an imposition. It is peaceful; it avoids violent methods; it is patient; it is generous.

3. Trust, not only in the power of one's words, but also in an attitude of welcoming the trust of the interlocutor. Trust promotes confidence and friendship. It binds hearts in mutual adherence to the good which excludes all self-seeking.

4. Finally, pedagogical prudence, which esteems highly the psychological and moral circumstances of the listener (cf. Mt

7:6) whether he be a child, uneducated, unprepared, diffident, hostile. Prudence strives to learn the sensitivities of the hearer and requires that we adapt ourselves and the manner of our presentation in a reasonable way lest we be displeasing and incomprehensible to him.

In the dialogue, conducted in this manner, the union of truth and charity, of understanding and love is achieved.

—*Ecclesiam Suam,* 1964

**The Pedagogy of Diversity**   In the dialogue one discovers how different are the ways which lead to the light of faith, and how it is possible to make them converge on the same goal. Even if these ways are divergent, they can become complementary by forcing our reasoning process out of the worn paths and by obliging it to deepen its research, to find fresh expressions.

The dialectic of this exercise of thought and of patience will make us discover elements of truth also in the opinions of others, it will force us to express our teaching with great fairness, and it will reward us for the work of having explained it in accordance with the objections of another or despite his slow assimilation of our teaching. The dialogue will make us wise; it will make us teachers.                    —*Ecclesiam Suam,* 1964

**Balancing Fidelity and Adaptation**   To what extent should the Church adapt itself to the historic and local circumstances in which its mission is exercised? How should it guard against the danger of a relativism which would falsify its moral and dogmatic truth? And yet, at the same time, how can it fit itself to approach all men so as to save all, according to the example of the Apostle: "I became all things to all men that I might save all"? (1 Cor 9:22).                    —*Ecclesiam Suam,* 1964

**The Incarnational Nature of Dialogue**   The world cannot be saved from the outside. As the Word of God became man, so must a man to a certain degree identify himself with the forms of life of those to whom he wishes to bring the message of Christ. Without invoking privileges which would but widen the separation, without employing unintelligible terminology, he must share the common way of life — provided that it is human and honorable — especially of the most humble, if he wishes to be listened to and understood.                    —*Ecclesiam Suam*, 1964

**The Heart of Dialogue**    And before speaking, it is necessary to listen, not only to a man's voice, but to his heart. A man must first be understood — and, where he merits it, agreed with. In the very act of trying to make ourselves pastors, fathers and teachers of men, we must make ourselves their brothers. The spirit of dialogue is friendship and, even more, is service. All this we must remember and strive to put into practice according to the example and commandment that Christ left to us (cf. Jn 13:14–17).                                        —*Ecclesiam Suam*, 1964

**Compromising the Dialogue**    But the danger remains. The apostle's art is a risky one. The desire to come together as brothers must not lead to a watering-down or subtracting from the truth. Our dialogue must not weaken our attachment to our faith. In our apostolate we cannot make vague compromises about the principles of faith and action on which our profession of Christianity is based.

An immoderate desire to make peace and sink differences at all costs is, fundamentally, a kind of skepticism about the power and content of the Word of God which we desire to preach. Only the man who is completely faithful to the teaching of Christ can be an apostle. And only he who lives his Christian life to the full can remain uncontaminated by the errors with which he comes into contact.                                        —*Ecclesiam Suam*, 1964

**The Universal Relevance of Dialogue**    Speaking in general on the role of partner in dialogue, a role which the Catholic Church must take up with renewed fervor today, we should like merely to observe that the Church must be ever ready to carry on the dialogue with all men of good will, within and without its own sphere.

There is no one who is a stranger to its heart, no one in whom its ministry has no interest. It has no enemies, except those who wish to be such. Its name of Catholic is not an idle title. Not in vain has it received the commission to foster in the world unity, love, and peace.                                    —*Ecclesiam Suam,* 1964

**Respect and Solidarity in Dialogue**   We share with the whole of mankind a common nature; human life with all its gifts and problems. In this primary universal reality we are ready to play our part, to acknowledge the deep-seated claims of its fundamental needs, to applaud the new, and sometimes sublime, expressions of its genius.                                —*Ecclesiam Suam,* 1964

**Building Up the Human through Dialogue**   Wherever men are trying to understand themselves and the world, we can communicate with them. Wherever the councils of nations come together to establish the rights and duties of man, we are honored when they allow us to take our seat among them. If there exists in men "a soul which is naturally Christian," we desire to show it our respect and to enter into conversation with it.

Our attitude in this, as we remind ourselves and everyone else, is, on the one hand, entirely disinterested. We have no temporal or political aim whatever. On the other hand, its purpose is to raise up and elevate to a supernatural and Christian level every good human value in the world. We are not civilization, but we promote it.                               —*Ecclesiam Suam,* 1964

**Atheism**   This is the most serious problem of our time. We are firmly convinced that the theory on which the denial of God is based is utterly erroneous.

This theory is not in keeping with the basic, undeniable requirements of thought. It deprives the reasonable order of the world of its genuine foundation. This theory does not provide human life with a liberating formula but with a blind dogma which degrades and saddens it. This theory destroys, at the root, any social system which attempts to base itself upon it. It does not bring freedom. It is a sham, attempting to quench the light of the living God.

**Understanding the Atheist**   But though we must speak firmly and clearly in declaring and defending religion and the human values which it proclaims and upholds, we are moved by our pastoral office to seek in the heart of the modern atheist the motives of his turmoil and denial.

His motives are many and complex, so that we must examine them with care if we are to answer them effectively. Some of them arise from the demand that divine things be presented in a worthier and purer way than is, perhaps, the case in certain imperfect forms of language and worship, which we ought to try to purify so that they express as perfectly and clearly as possible the sacred reality of which they are the sign....

Sometimes, too, the atheist is spurred on by noble sentiments and by impatience with the mediocrity and self-seeking of so many contemporary social settings. He knows well how to borrow from our Gospel modes and expressions of solidarity and human compassion. Shall we not be able to lead him back one day to the Christian source of such manifestations of moral worth?                                        — *Ecclesiam Suam,* 1964

**Interfaith Dialogue**    Indeed, honesty compels us to declare openly our conviction that there is but one true religion, the religion of Christianity. It is our hope that all who seek God and adore Him may come to acknowledge its truth.

But we do, nevertheless, recognize and respect the moral and spiritual values of the various non-Christian religions, and we desire to join with them in promoting and defending common ideals of religious liberty, human brotherhood, good culture, social welfare and civil order. For our part, we are ready to enter into discussion on these common ideals, and will not fail to take the initiative where our offer of discussion in genuine, mutual respect, would be well received.        — *Ecclesiam Suam,* 1964

**Ecumenical Dialogue**    The principle that we are happy to make our own is this: Let us stress what we have in common rather than what divides us. This provides a good and fruitful subject for our dialogue. We are ready to carry it out wholeheartedly. We will say more: On many points of difference regarding tradition, spirituality, canon law, and worship, we are ready to study how we can satisfy the legitimate desires of our Christian brothers, still separated from us. It is our dearest wish to embrace them in a perfect union of faith and charity.

But we must add that it is not in our power to compromise with the integrity of the faith or the requirements of charity. We foresee that this will cause misgiving and opposition, but now that the Catholic Church has taken the initiative in restoring the unity of Christ's fold, it will not cease to go forward with all patience and consideration.

It will not cease to show that the prerogatives, which keep the separated brothers at a distance, are not the fruits of historic ambition or of fanciful theological speculation, but derive from the will of Christ and that, rightly understood, they are for the good of all and make for common unity, freedom and Christian perfection. The Catholic Church will not cease, by prayer and penance, to prepare herself worthily for the longed-for reconciliation.                                                —*Ecclesiam Suam,* 1964

## *Conclusion*

It would be difficult to find a more suitable topic than dialogue through which to introduce *lectio divina. Lectio divina* is essentially a dialogical, interactive process. We communicate with God, ourselves, and potentially others (when practiced in a group setting), and can also discover His word / initiative in nature and life. When I teach *lectio divina* in secular environments as a model of healing and communications, I describe the prayer and contemplation stages as active and receptive dialogue.

The same principles operative in spiritual dialogue as modeled by Paul VI are present in *lectio divina,* for example, patience, receptivity, honesty, responsiveness, and discernment.

In *lectio divina* we encounter God's word, primarily in Scripture, but it can also be manifested in other ways articulated or anticipated by Scripture. For example, in other persons, particularly those who are vulnerable or suffering (cf. Mt 25:34–40), in significant life events (manifestations of divine signs, or God's initiative in our lives), in Scripture-rooted sources like the sacraments, spiritual classics, and Church teachings (e.g., Pope Paul's).

We can also integrate *lectio divina* with another discernment and communications activity, journaling. And of course, since Jesus is the primary manifestation of God's word (cf. Jn 1:1–18; 1 Jn 1:1–4), any interaction with God can be an opportunity to experience the model of *lectio divina.*

*Lectio divina* was originally described within the early Church in terms of two activities, reading and prayer, which encompassed meditation and contemplation as well. Meditation and contemplation were spelled out later as the desert fathers and early monastics reflected further on the Bible reading process. During the Middle Ages, the stage of action was added, in large part due to the influence of Richard of St. Victor.

In my other books I explain the origins, development, process, and applications of *lectio divina* in detail. However, because it is such an instinctive and fundamental activity, it can also be explained concisely and learned by doing.

The stages of reading, meditation, prayer, contemplation, and action are a concise description of both spirituality and communication, and therefore we should view them as a whole as well as individual parts. They constitute the natural way people communicate and practice spirituality. They are inherent in spiritual practices and living, even for non-Christians.

Many believers, including non Catholic Christians, instinctively go through the process of *lectio divina* while interacting with God and the Scriptures. Of course, the stages and process as a whole has distinct connotations, contexts, and applications for Christians, but there is also a generic human element.

The experience of *lectio* is rich and there are many subtleties, nuances, depths, opportunities, and applications associated with it, but in its basic manifestation it is rather simple: If our subject of *lectio divina* is the Bible or another spiritual text (including an entry in our journal), we read a small portion (no minimum amount to cover) until we encounter something that speaks to us, which in *lectio divina* we refer to as a word. We then repeat it to internalize it, reflect on it to assimilate it, and relate it to our experience or other texts in order to discover its personal significance. This is the meditation stage.

The emotional and spiritual response evoked by these activities is the dialogue referred to as prayer and contemplation. We speak and listen, back and forth as in an ordinary conversation. *Lectio* is interactive and fluid rather than linear and mechanical. It's not like we proceed through the stages in perfect order according to a preordained pattern. Human communications aren't like that.

Rather, we oscillate between the stages according to the movement of the Spirit within us. We don't necessarily start at the beginning. Perhaps the Spirit initially draws us to prayer and contemplation, or even action, e.g., responding to a human need, which is a Christological (cf. Mt 25:31–46) manifestation of God's word.

In prayer we share our emotional and spiritual response to God's word, how it affects us and perhaps our relationships. In contemplation, we sit quietly and expectantly, waiting on God in the words of the psalmists (cf. Ps 27:14; 33:20; 62:1, 5; 130:4–5). Traditionally contemplation has been referred to as simple presence. We give God a chance to get a word in edgewise. It's the cooling down stage of the process, relaxing our energies and allowing the Spirit to blow where it will (cf. Jn 3:8).

Action is where we implement and live the word we receive. We don't read the Bible or Paul VI just for education or edification. It is meant to evoke a response in us, to enlighten, heal, build up, and transform, and to inspire us to reach out to others and share what we have received. *Lectio* is a dynamic, contagious activity that bridges the spiritual and apostolic life. Because Paul's teachings draw extensively from Scripture and life, they are a natural source for *lectio*.

*Lectio divina* is therefore a fitting model for entering into a dialogue with Paul's words. Let us enter this dialogue in a natural, relaxed manner, just as we would a conversation.

# Chapter 5

# Peace

*And now our message reaches its highest point, which is, at first, a negative point. You are expecting us to utter this sentence, and we are well aware of its gravity and solemnity: not the ones against the others, never again, never more. It was principally for this purpose that the organization of the United Nations arose: against war, in favor of peace.*

*Listen to the lucid words of the great departed John Kennedy, who proclaimed four years ago, "Mankind must put an end to war or war will put an end to mankind."*

*Many words are not needed to proclaim this loftiest aim of your institution. It suffices to remember that the blood of millions of men, that numberless and unheard-of sufferings, useless slaughter and frightful ruin are the sanction of the pact which unites you, with an oath which must change the future history of the world: No more war, war never again. Peace, it is peace which must guide the destinies of people and of all mankind.* —Pope Paul VI, Address to the U.N. General Assembly, October 4, 1965

As an adolescent I had two main images of Paul VI. The first came from my mother, who would "invite" me to clean off my plate out of respect for the starving folks in India, and remind me that their suffering had even brought the pope to tears on his visit to Calcutta in 1964. The second image is Paul's magnificent speech at the United Nations and his action-packed whirlwind trip to New York City on October 4, 1965. That year, he outdrew another famous Paul (McCartney) and his mates. The Beatles attracted a record fifty-five thousand fans to their historic Shea Stadium concert, while

Paul VI drew ninety thousand to his Mass for Peace at Yankee Stadium.

I remember reading accounts of Paul's U.N. speech centered on his gripping mantra, "no more war, war never again"! (John Paul II periodically cited this phrase in his peacemaking efforts.) This led me to seek out the numerous books that chronicled Paul's trip and the texts of his speeches. So many were printed that forty years later it is not uncommon to run across them at a used book sale.

Paul's homily at Yankee Stadium centered on peace in a Mass designated for peace. Ours is a God of peace (cf. Rom 15:33; 16:20; 1 Cor 14:33), and peace is Jesus' gift to us (cf. Jn 14:27; 16:33; 20:21, 26). We would do well to make every Mass a Mass for peace, seeking reconciliation and an end to violence as a response to our reception of the Lord in his word, body and blood, and in each other.

Politically, the 1960s was one of the bloodiest decades in modern times. In the United States, three major assassinations (President Kennedy, Senator Robert Kennedy, Reverend Dr. Martin Luther King Jr.) changed the political and social landscape. Civil wars erupted throughout Asia and Africa. The geography and politics of the Middle East was dramatically altered by the 1967 conflict between Israel and Egypt. The Vietnam War sparked civil unrest that toppled a president (Johnson) and undermined the social and economic stability of the United States for a decade, with residual effects to this day.

Amid the chaos there were many voices for peace in all parts of society — in popular culture (the peace movement promoted by activists, poets, and musicians), volunteer groups such as the Peace Corps, and populist politicians such as Senator Eugene McCarthy, an unsuccessful Democratic candidate for president in 1968.

Paul VI not only preached, but also lived the message of peace. Peace and dialogue go together. When Paul met opposition within the Church, he sought to convince rather than coerce. He was extraordinarily patient and tolerant of those who questioned his teachings and lobbied for change, even schismatic forces like Archbishop Lefebvre and his followers, who rejected Vatican II reforms.

I would like to contrast the peace initiatives of Paul VI with those of the peaceniks, the anti-war youth culture. It is both admirable and helpful to use music, art, poetry, drama, and mass protests in the cause of peace, but attitudes and actions are what ultimately effect change. Public chants of "give peace a chance" raise awareness and enthusiasm, but of themselves do not change the heart, the area in which Paul specialized.

While the peaceniks' sentiments and objectives may have been similar to Paul's, there was a vast difference in their intellectual, theological, and moral underpinnings. When we read Paul's teachings on peace, we immediately discover that we are not being fed naive, idealistic jingoism. We are not encountering nice-sounding phrases rooted more in ideology than reality. Paul's appeal for peace was couched in the universal language of brotherhood, but it was also based upon ascetical, theological, and moral principles that recognized human weakness and peace's dependence on such virtues and values as dialogue, self-discipline, and human development.

In Paul's mind, peace is born of ongoing conversion and obedience to the dictates of faith and conscience. It is not an egocentric and entertaining endeavor. The first place violence must be met is within. Peacemaking, like politics, is local. The first conflict in the Bible is within Cain and then between brothers.

We first must be at peace with ourselves and our neighbor before we can lobby effectively for global peace. We have to be messengers of peace in word and deed, in the concrete actions and decisions of life, including in situations where violence disguises itself in socially acceptable forms such as gossip, slander, calumny, false witness, character assassination, salaciousness, lust, malicious lawsuits, and legal posturing. As the popular song goes, peace has to begin with me.

Amid the disapproval of peers and the masses, am I willing to pay a price and make sacrifices for my peacemaking?

Like the other beatitudes, the one on peacemaking regards suffering as a predecessor to divine reward. Paradoxically, Jesus inaugurated a kingdom of peace that undergoes violence (cf. Mt 11:12), epitomized by his suffering and death.

Am I willing to be passionate for peace, not just on the emotional and ideological level, but by following in the footsteps of Jesus and living it in daily encounters?

# PEACE

**We Must Love Peace**    First of all, you must love peace. Here we can use the words of Christ: "Blessed are the peacemakers, for they shall be called the sons of God" (Mt 5:9) If we truly wish to be Christians, we must love peace, we must make our own the cause of peace, we must meditate on the real meaning of peace, we must conform our minds to the thought of peace.

—Homily at Mass for Peace, Yankee Stadium, October 4, 1965

**We Must Work for Peace**    You must serve the cause of peace. Serve it, and not make use of it for aims other than the true aims of peace. Serve it, and not use this noble standard as a cover for cowardice or selfishness, which refuses to make sacrifices for the common good; nor debilitate and pervert the spirit, by evading the call of duty and seeking one's own interests and pleasure.    —Homily at Mass for Peace, Yankee Stadium, October 4, 1965

**Peace Is Spiritual**    Peace must be based on moral and religious principles, which will make it sincere and stable. Politics do not suffice to sustain a durable peace. The absence of conflict does not suffice to make of peace a source of happiness and of true human progress.

—Homily at Mass for Peace, Yankee Stadium, October 4, 1965

**The Wisdom Underlying Peace**    Peace must have its roots anchored in wisdom, and this wisdom must draw nourishment from the true concept of life, that is, the Christian concept....

**The Peace of Christ**    Jesus, the Prince of Peace (Is 9:6), has His own original and characteristic peace, which can regulate every human relationship because, in the very first place, it regulates the relationship with God.

—Homily at Mass for Peace, Yankee Stadium, October 4, 1965

**The New Name for Peace Is Development**    Peace cannot be limited to a mere absence of war, the result of an ever precarious balance of forces. No, peace is something that is built up day after day, in the pursuit of an order intended by God, which implies a more perfect form of justice among men.... For, if the new name for peace is development, who would not wish to labor for it with all his powers?  —*Populorum Progressio,* 1967

**Peace Is a Gift**   Yes, peace is a gift from God. It requires His beneficial, merciful and mysterious intervention. But His gift is not always a miraculous one. It is a gift which works its wonders in the recess of men's hearts, and hence it is a gift requiring ready acceptance and cooperation on our part. And so, after directing our prayer to heaven, we direct it to men all over the world.
—Fiftieth Anniversary Celebration
of the Fatima Apparitions, May 13, 1967

**The Root of Peace Is Obedience**   And how could we speak of peace without referring to the principle that produces, inside and outside us, the order that generates and ensures peace, that is obedience?  —Papal audience, October 16, 1968

**The Progressive Nature of Peace**   Fortunately another set of ideals and facts appears before our gaze; and it is that of progressive peace. For, notwithstanding everything, peace marches on. There are breaks in continuity, there are inconsistencies and difficulties. But all the same peace marches on and is establishing itself in the world with a certain invincibility. Every man is conscious of it: peace is necessary.

It has in its favor the moral progress of humanity, which is indisputably directed toward unity. Unity and peace, when freedom unites them, are sisters.
—Day of Peace Message, November 14, 1970

**Love Brings Peace**   Let us venture to use a word, which may itself appear ambiguous, but which, given the thought its deep significance demands, is ever splendid and supreme. The word is "love": love for man, as the highest principle of the terrestrial order.

Love and peace are correlative entities. Peace is a product of love: true love, human love.
—Day of Peace Message, November 14, 1970

**Peace Presupposes Friendship**    Peace supposes a certain "identity of choice": this is friendship. If we want peace, we must recognize the necessity of building it upon foundations more substantial than the non-existence of relations (relations among men are inevitable; they grow and become necessary), or the existence of self-interest (these are precarious and often deceptive), or the web of purely cultural or fortuitous relations (these can be double-edged, for peace or for combat.

—Day of Peace Message, November 14, 1970

**Peace and Brotherhood**    True peace must be founded upon justice, upon a sense of the intangible dignity of man, upon the recognition of an abiding and happy equality between men, upon the basic principle of human brotherhood, that is, of the respect and love due to each man, because he is man.

The victorious word springs forth: because he is a brother. My brother, our brother.    —Day of Peace Message, November 14, 1970

**Brotherhood Breeds Peace**    This consciousness of a universal human brotherhood is also happily developing in our world, at least in principle.... Where brotherhood amongst men is at root disregarded, peace is at root destroyed.

And yet peace is the mirror of the real, authentic, modern humanity, victorious over every anachronistic self-injury. Peace is the great concept extolling love amongst men who discover that they are brothers and decide to live as such....

"Treat others as you would like them to treat you; that is the meaning of the Law and the Prophets" (Mt 7:12). How philosophers and saints have meditated on this maxim, which implants the universality of the precept of brotherhood into the individual and positive actions of social morality!...

And so, finally, we are in a position to provide the supreme argument: the concept of God's Fatherhood, among all men, proclaimed to all believers. A true brotherhood, among men, to be authentic and binding presupposes and demands a transcendental Fatherhood overflowing with metaphysical love and supernatural charity.    —Day of Peace Message, November 14, 1970

**Reconciliation and Peace**   We know that we shall find the way to God's altar barred if we have not first removed the obstacle to reconciliation with our brother man (Mt 5:23ff., 6:14–15).

And we know that if we are Promoters of peace, then we can be called sons of God, and be among those whom the Gospel calls blessed (Mt 5:9).

What strength, what fruitfulness, what confidence the Christian religion bestows on the equation of brotherhood and peace. What joy it is for us to find, at the meeting point of these two terms, the crossing of the paths of our faith with those of the hopes of humanity and civilization.

— Day of Peace Message, November 14, 1970

**Reconciliation Is a Peace Offering**   The duty of making peace extends personally to each and every member of the faithful. If it is not fulfilled, even the sacrifice of worship which they intend to offer (Mt 5.23ff.) remains ineffective.

Mutual reconciliation, in fact, shares in the very value of the sacrifice itself, and together with it constitutes a single offering pleasing to God.   — Papal audience, December 8, 1974

**Peace Can Conquer Violence**   How true it is that if all men of good will throughout the world could be mobilized in a concerted effort for peace, the tragic temptation to resort to violence could then be overcome.

— Conference of the Food and Agriculture Organization,
November 16, 1970

**Peace Is Dynamic**   Peace is not a stagnant condition of life which finds in it at the same time both its perfection and its death. Life is movement, growth, work, effort and conquest, things such as these.

Is that what Peace is like? Yes, for the very reason that it coincides with the supreme good of man as he makes his way through time, and this good is never attained totally, but is always being newly and inexhaustibly acquired. Peace is thus the central idea giving its driving force to the most active enthusiasm.   — Papal audience, December 8, 1971

**Peace Is Dynamic**   The certainty of Peace is based not only on being but also on becoming. Like man's life, Peace is dynamic. Its realm extends more and principally into the field of moral obligation, that is, into the sphere of duties. Peace must not only be maintained; it must be produced. Therefore Peace is, and must always be, in a process of continuous and progressive realization.                    —Celebration of the Day of Peace, January 1, 1974

**Peace through Justice**   Peace is something very human.... If we look for its true source, we find that it is rooted in a sincere feeling for man. A Peace that is not the result of true respect for man is not true Peace. And what do we call this sincere feeling for man? We call it justice....

The invitation we gave to celebrate Peace resounds as an invitation to practice Justice: "Justice will bring about Peace" (cf. Is 32:17). We repeat this today in a more incisive and dynamic formula: "If you want Peace, work for Justice."

—Papal audience, December 8, 1971

**Linking Peace, Progress, and Love**   "Development is the new name of peace," we wrote at the end of the encyclical *Populorum Progressio*; and this name is the equivalent of charity.

The Church is called to work for peace and progress; in the love that springs from the Heart of Christ She knows full well that it is to Christ, hidden in the least of the brethren, that go all the most hidden and humble attentions paid to those who are hungry, thirsty, lacking clothing and shelter, sick and imprisoned (cf. Mt 25:31–46), to the uneducated and despised, the humiliated, the oppressed, those who are thrust aside because of ethnic or racial prejudices.

"...It is time for all men and all peoples to face up to their responsibilities." Upon this road the Church is on the side of all those who take unselfishly to heart the destiny of mankind.

—Papal audience, June 22, 1973

**Love Is Our Inner Peace**   Where and how to find peace, integration, balance, the fullness of our personality? The answer is at hand: love is our inner peace. The question then arises: what love? ...

To be happy it is necessary to learn "the art of loving." It is an art in which nature itself is a master, if listened to carefully and interpreted according to the great and sovereign law of love, as taught us by Christ: love God, love your neighbor, with the strict and vital applications that this law entails.

If we really learned to love as we should, would not our personal life, and consequently our collective life be transformed into peace and happiness?  —Papal audience, October 17, 1973

**World Peace Is Possible**  Even today we are experiencing a painful event of war, and not the only one. We are humiliated and frightened.

It is possible that this is an incurable disease of mankind? We should also point out here the congenital disproportion in mankind between its capacity of idealization and its moral aptitude to remain consistent and faithful to its programs of civil progress.

Thus one is tempted to say: it is impossible for the world to remain at peace. We answer: no; Christ, our peace (Eph 2:14), makes the impossible possible (cf. Lk 18:27). If we follow his Gospel, the union of justice and peace can be realized; certainly not to be crystallized in the immobility of a history that is, on the contrary, in continual development: but it is possible! It can be reborn! ...

Why is it not possible to conceive a human society, in which interests are certainly different and conflicting, but which is based on organic and just cooperation, and therefore on the human and Christian peace of all those who constitute it?

Are these dreams? Madness? This is our originality; we believe that this political eschatology, this moral parousia, is a Christian duty, whatever may be the degree of its actual application in the historical situation. Love, justice, peace are living and good ideals, full of social energy, which we must not change into hatred and conflict, in order to aim at that concrete peace

that will realize in wisdom and goodness Christ's words: "you
are all brothers" (Mt 23:8).        —Papal audience, October 17, 1973

**Peace Is an Ethical Priority**   We shall go further and say:
Peace is possible only if it is considered a duty. It is not even
enough that it be based on the conviction, in general perfectly justified, that it is advantageous. Peace must take hold
of the consciences of men as a supreme ethical objective, as a
moral necessity... deriving from the innate demands of human
coexistence.        —Celebration of the Day of Peace, January 1, 1974

**The Concept of Peace**   Peace is above all an idea. It is an inner
axiom and a treasure of the spirit. Peace must grow out of a
fundamentally spiritual concept of humanity: humanity must be
at Peace, that is, united and consistent in itself, closely bound
together in the depth of its being.
  The absence of this basic concept has been, and still is, the
root cause of the calamities which have devastated history. To
regard struggle among men as a structural need of society is
not only an error of philosophy and vision but also a potential
and permanent crime against humanity.
                 —Celebration of the Day of Peace, January 1, 1974

**Peace Depends on Me**   Peace is possible, if each one of us
wants it; if each one of us loves Peace, educates and forms his
own outlook to Peace, defends Peace, works for Peace. Each
one of us must listen in his own conscience to the impelling
call: "Peace depends on you too."...
  Peace has need of you. If you want to, you can succeed. Peace
depends also and especially on you....
  It is a wonderful thing: Peace is possible, and furthermore it
depends, through Christ our Peace (Eph 2:4), on us. May our
Apostolic Blessing of Peace be a pledge thereof.
                 —Celebration of the Day of Peace, January 1, 1974

**Christ Our Peace**   God, in fact, has not simply pardoned us,
nor has He made use of a mere man as an intermediary between
us and Himself: He has established His "only begotten Son an
intercessor of peace."

For our sake God made the sinless one into sin so that in him we might become the goodness of God" (2 Cor 5:21). In reality, Christ, by dying for us, has canceled out "every record of the debt that we had to pay; he has done away with it by nailing it to the cross" (Col 2:14). And by means of the Cross He has reconciled us with God: "In his own person he has killed the hostility" (Eph 2:16). —Papal audience, December 8, 1974

**Make Peace with Yourself First**   Once reconciliation has been received, it is, like grace and like life, an impulse and a current that transforms their beneficiaries into agents and transmitters of the same reconciliation. For every Christian the credential of his authenticity in the Church and in the world is this: "First make peace with yourself, so that when you have become peaceful you may bring peace to others."
—Papal audience, December 8, 1974

**The First Fruit of the Redemption Is Peace**   Reconciliation, in its double aspect of peace restored between God and men and between man and man, is the first fruit of the Redemption, and like the Redemption has dimensions that are universal both in extent and in intensity. The whole of creation, therefore, is involved in reconciliation "till the universal restoration comes" (Acts 3:21), when all creatures will again meet Christ, the "first to be born from the dead" (Col 1:18).
—Papal audience, December 8, 1974

**Peace and Sacrifice Foster Unity and Personality Development**
Since our reconciliation springs from the sacrifice of Christ who freely died for us, may the cross . . . inspire our mutual relations so that they may all be truly Christian. Let none of these relations ever lack some personal renunciation. From this there will follow a fraternal openness to others such as will allow willing recognition of each one's abilities and will permit all to make their proper contribution to the enrichment of the one ecclesial communion: "Thus through the common sharing of gifts and through the common effort to attain fullness in unity, the whole and each of the parts receive increase." In this sense, one can

agree on the fact that unity, properly understood, permits each individual to develop his own personality.

— Papal audience, December 8, 1974

**Peace and Dialogue**    Peace is possible, peace is a duty for us, peace is necessary. There is entering into the conscience of peoples the firm and decided conviction that it is impossible to construct anything effective and lasting for the good of man unless in mutual concord, in respect of reciprocal rights, in the patient experiment of constructive talks and just and sincere negotiations.

And looking at what is happening on this day on which — as its joyful and ever wider echoes reach us every year — in the capitals of the various states of the world, at the seats of the international organizations, in ecclesial communities, civil and religious leaders stop for a pause of meditated reflection, nay more, of common prayer, then deep joy fills our heart. Here we have the real arms of peace, which is gaining ground, though with difficulty and slowly, and progressing in the hearts of men enlightened by God's light.        — Papal audience, January 1, 1976

**Peace Begins with Me**    We are all responsible for peace, we are all called to collaborate for peace, making our personal contribution to the building-up of a society based on love, in our environment, our profession, and daily relations. We are all called to fight with the powerful arms of love and brotherhood for the establishment, safeguarding and diffusion of peace around us. Let each one begin by himself; the number will grow enormously; it is a work to which no one must remain extraneous.                                — Papal audience, January 1, 1976

**Prayer for Peace**    We entrust these ardent wishes to the wisdom and goodness of Him who is the Prince of Peace. May He strengthen good dispositions with His grace. And we also entrust our hopes to her who, showing Him to the world as the Author of peace, can implore from Him upon humanity the great, indispensable gift of real peace. May the holy Mother of God answer us mercifully in this way, on this first day of the year, dedicated to her; may she accompany us in this way for the days which we are awaiting. Amen, amen.

—Papal audience, January 1, 1976

## Conclusion

*Lectio divina* is a peaceful process and therefore is an excellent model for interacting with Paul's witness in word and deed on the subject of peace. It is a fluid activity, serenely and naturally interactive, though as in the case of peacemaking it can have some unsettling aspects.

Spiritual peace is not always accompanied by calm and emotional tranquility. Since as in St. Paul's description (cf. Phil 4:7) it is beyond understanding, we cannot expect it to conform to our expectations or familiar experiences.

*Lectio* is a good model for peacemaking because it is holistic, involving the senses (reading aloud, for example, engages sight, hearing, speaking, touch, and, in the metaphorical language of the monks, tasting the word of God; cf. Ps 34:8; 119:103). *Lectio* engages the mind, senses, emotions, and spirit. Peacemaking has to be an activity of the whole person in order to be fully credible to others, particularly those inclined to aggression and violence and thereby resistant to superficial measures.

Peace parallels *lectio* in that it is a process that transcends feelings. It is a graced disposition, a state of being, a gift from God just as His word is. Peacemakers seek specific outcomes but are not obsessed with them. Providence has the final word.

Likewise when we engage in *lectio,* we have particular results that we seek (e.g., peace of mind, a sense of God's presence and providence, discernment of spirits with respect to a decision, personal and relationship transformation), but ultimately we leave the outcome in God's hands, entrusting it to His wisdom and mercy. In the spirit of the Hebrew greeting and word for peace, *shalom,* which also means wholeness or well-being, we engage Paul and more importantly God, ourselves, and others in search of harmony and reconciliation.

# Chapter 6

# Faith

*In a word, then, the edifice of modern civilization must be built upon spiritual principles which alone can, not only support it, but even illuminate and animate it. To do this, such indispensable principles of superior wisdom cannot but be founded — so, as you are aware, we believe — upon faith in God.*

*That unknown God, of whom St. Paul spoke to the Athenians in the Areopagus, unknown by them, although without realizing it they sought Him and He was close to them, as happens also to many men of our times. To us, in any case, and to all those who accept the ineffable revelation which Christ has given us of Him, He is the living God, the Father of all men.* — Pope Paul VI, Address to the U.N. General Assembly, October 4, 1965

Faith is an ambiguous term to many people. Not to Paul VI. In fact, he gave us a comprehensive definition, a creed no less, a profession of faith known as the "Credo" of the People of God, issued on July 30, 1968. Unfortunately, few paid attention.

Unlike John Paul's catechism, which was accompanied by much anticipation, publicity, and support, Paul's creed was barely noticed, much less heeded. A telling difference between their catechetical approaches is the level of detail offered in their instruction. Paul VI offered the foundation of a creed and invited the faithful to fill in the gaps with sound Catholic spirituality and doctrine. John Paul provided much of that for us, leaving little to discretion and interpretation.

Likewise in the area of sexuality, Paul VI communicated general principles and counsels through an encyclical and periodic addresses, whereas over a period of five years (1979–84) John Paul used his weekly audiences to present a corpus of doctrine known as the "theology of the body." In subsequent years he would concentrate on topics such as each person of the Trinity and develop them in detail.

Paul's creed is important for three reasons. First, it reveals the pontiff's mind with regards to the central tenets of the Church's faith in language and concepts accessible to modern persons. The pope is giving us an example of how to balance tradition and orthodoxy with contemporary pastoral concerns.

Second, it provides a much needed balance to the moral focus prevalent today. We have to be concerned with theological, catechetical, social justice, and spirituality issues as well as morality. Catholicism is an integrated balance of all dimensions of Christian faith.

Third, it complements the *Catechism of the Catholic Church*. Many Catholics don't have the time to read the *Catechism* in detail or the theological background to comprehend it sufficiently. Paul's creed is more accessible and manageable.

Because it presents core teachings in a traditional framework according to contemporary sensitivities, the creed is as relevant today as in 1968. Like the Nicene Creed recited at Mass, each line is amenable to reflection, study, and prayer. Excerpts from the creed relating to the Trinity and selected other doctrines are presented in the chapter.

Paul VI's perspective on faith is not static or abstract. It combines content (the creed and other catechetical instruction) with personal assent to form a dynamic, lived experience.

St. Paul's discussion of faith in Romans and Galatians is often misinterpreted to be a purely notional reality. St. Paul frequently refers to faith working itself out through love — a theme also emphasized in the Epistle of James (cf. Jas 2:14–26), which sought to correct misunderstandings of St. Paul's teaching on salvation by faith alone.

Pope Paul's comments on faith in this chapter serve a dual role. They remind us of what we believe and the applications and response that should follow. Pope Benedict has frequently warned of the dangers of reducing Christian faith to humanistic considerations. Pope

Paul's teachings touch us at the level of the intellect, will, emotions, and spirit, helping us to bring our whole selves to God in the process of developing and living out our faith.

## *FAITH*

**The Precise Science of Theology**  Having safeguarded the integrity of the faith, it is necessary to safeguard also its proper mode of expression, lest by the careless use of words, we occasion (God forbid) the rise of false opinions regarding faith in the most sublime of mysteries. St. Augustine gives a stern warning about this in his consideration of the way of speaking employed by the philosophers and of that which ought to be used by Christians.

St. Augustine: "The philosophers," he says, "speak freely without fear of offending religious listeners on subjects quite difficult to understand. We, on the other hand, must speak according to a fixed norm, lest the lack of restraint in our speech result in some impious opinion even about the things signified by the words themselves." — *Mysterium Fidei,* 1965

**Faith Works with Reason**  Faith has need of the intellect; it gives confidence to the intelligence, respects it, requires it, defends it; and by the very fact that it involves the study of divine truth, it obliges the intelligence to an absolute honesty in thought and to an effort that, far from weakening it, strengthens it in the natural as well as the supernatural order of inquiry.
— Papal audience, June 5, 1968

**Faith Flows into Action**  Neither is it true that Faith is a bar to action; here again the very contrary is true. Faith requires action; it is a dynamic principle of morality (*iustus ex fide vivit*); the just man draws his very life from Faith.... Faith demands action, expresses itself in charity, that is in works, moved thereto by the love of God and of the neighbor.
— Papal audience, June 5, 1968

**Faith Is Not a Crutch**    In the same way there is no foundation for that unworthy rejection of Faith, as though it were an artificial soporific for human suffering and a false myth which separates man from the realities of life. Nay; it is truth, splendid and consoling, for it reveals to us the wonderful designs of divine goodness. It is not meant to lull man to sleep in the midst of his dangers and toils, but to make him aware of them and to give him the energy to sustain them with manly fortitude.

—Papal audience, June 5, 1968

**Faith Leads to Salvation**    That is what Faith means; it takes away that despair, that skepticism, that rebelliousness with which modern man, no longer supported by Faith, is plagued; instead it gives him the meaning of life and of its affairs, gives him hope in wise and honest activity, gives him strength to suffer and to love. Yes indeed; Faith does serve some purpose, and what a purpose — our salvation!        —Papal audience, June 5, 1968

**Charity Is the Fulfillment of Faith**    Remember the words of St. Paul: "Fides quae per caritatem operatur," faith operating by means of charity (Gal 5:6).

The theologians tell us that charity is the fulfillment of faith, that is to say, gives Faith that full quality which makes it firm and directs it efficaciously toward its purpose, which is God, sought, desired, loved, possessed through love. Thus "charity is called the form of faith, insofar as through the medium of charity the act of faith is integrated and completed."

—Papal audience, June 19, 1968

**Faith Must Be Personal**    Faith must be for us a personal fact, a conscious act, willed and deep. This subjective element of faith is most important today; it has always been necessary, because it is part and parcel of the authentic act of faith, but often it has been and is still substituted for by tradition, by historic environment, by common custom.

Today it is indispensable. Each one has to express in himself his personal faith with great awareness and great energy.

—Papal audience, June 19, 1968

**Live Your Faith**    But there is another consequence deriving from a profession of faith; it is the coherence of life with faith itself. We have never given enough importance to this close relation between believing and living.

It is not sufficient to know the Word of God; it has to be lived. To know the faith and not apply it to life would be gravely illogical, would be a serious responsibility. The faith is a principle of supernatural life, and at the same time it is a principle of moral life.                                    —Papal audience, July 3, 1968

**Faith Is Based on Truth**    Faith is not fideism, that is, belief deprived of rational grounds. It is not merely the subconscious search for some religious experience; it is possession of truth, it is certainty. "If your eye is not sound, your whole body will be full of darkness" (Mt 6:23).        —Papal audience, October 30, 1968

**Faith Is a Grace**    This dramatic situation of faith nowadays reminds us of the wise pronouncement of the council: "Sacred Tradition, holy Scripture and the Magisterium of the Church are, by the wise disposition of God, so closely connected with one another that they cannot exist independently."

This is all right for objective faith; that is, to know exactly what we must believe. But for subjective faith, what shall we do, after having listened, studied and meditated honestly and assiduously? Shall we have faith?

We can answer affirmatively, but always keeping in mind a fundamental and, in a certain sense, tremendous aspect of the question — that faith is a grace. "They have not all heeded the Gospel," St. Paul says (Rom 10:16).

—Papal audience, October 30, 1968

**Treasuring and Seeking the Gift of Faith**    And so, what about us? Shall we be among the fortunate ones to possess the gift of faith? Certainly, but it is a gift that we must treasure, guard, enjoy and practice in our lives. And therefore we must implore it in prayer, like the man in the Gospel: "I believe, help my unbelief" (Mk 9:24).                                      —Papal audience, October 30, 1968

**Science and Sensory Experience as a Barrier to Faith**   Modern man has, more than man in the past, the need and the ability to get in touch with the mystery of God, but he is not as ready as his ancestors to meet and admit this necessary and inevitable mystery, because he has widened the scope of his study and observation; and he is therefore tempted to feel satisfied with what he knows scientifically and through the senses.

—Papal audience, November 13, 1968

**Realism Contrasted with Pessimism**   We must enter the realistic vision of faith, which shows us the inevitable inability of man to be good and just, when left to himself and unaided. It is not only our catechism that tells us so. A large part of modern literature and of films and plays today provide despairing documentary evidence on this point.

The pessimism that prevails in art steeped in modern psychology tells us even more eloquently than the religious teacher how sick man is in the innermost recesses of his existence, how he dreams and struggles in vain to reach happiness and the fullness of his being, how inexorably he betrays his moral insufficiency and his inner corruption, and how he feels, condemned to skepticism, despair, nothingness.

—Papal audience, March 4, 1970

**Living by Faith and Grace**   In other words, the Christian lives by an inheritance, on a memory which comes down from a past historical event which was decisive for the destiny of mankind: the Gospel; he also lives in the present which is communicated to him by the Holy Spirit from a sphere beyond time and natural reality. This is to say that he lives by faith and grace. If this line should break, man's life as a Christian is extinguished. It is a matter of life and death.          —Papal audience, May 27, 1970

**Faith's Relationship with Hope**   But let Us say at once: this link with the past and with the transcendent supernatural does not draw the believer away from the present and from the future, in time and in the other world, but on the contrary draws him more deeply into them.

How is this? It is so because the faith to which he assents is a promise by its very nature. Rather, it is assent to truths which have still to be completely revealed to our knowledge and enjoyed by us. How does the letter to the Hebrews describe faith? It uses that celebrated formula: "Faith is the substance of things hoped for, the certainty of things not yet seen" (Heb 11:1). Therefore faith has an essential relationship with hope.

—Papal audience, May 27, 1970

**Consistency Underlies Authenticity**   Hence the great norms of Christian life: logic, consistency, faithfulness. Having admitted a principle, one must have the clearsightedness and the energy to draw its consequences.

The Christian is a consistent man, a man of "character." "The righteous man, St. Paul says further, finds life through faith" (Gal 3:11). Not just *with* faith, but *through* faith.

This consistency qualifies the authenticity of the Christian. To be decorated with this name without complying with its requirements is deceitfulness, pharisaism, maybe utilitarianism and conformism.                                  —Papal audience, June 16, 1971

**Interior/Subjective and External/Objective Principles of Faith**
We all know that Christian life is a way of conceiving and leading life according to faith (Rom 1:17; Gal 3:11; Heb 10:38). Now, faith has two principles, one interior and operating, and it is the virtue of faith, the disposition to believe, which comes from the Holy Spirit and is infused in us with baptism; the other external and determining, made up of the positive truths to believe, taught us by the Church, in the "creed," that is in the "symbol" (which means synthesis, summary) of the same truths — the catechism.                              —Papal audience, September 22, 1971

**Science and Wisdom Can Be Complementary**   We have neglected the ways of wisdom to follow the ways of science. Not that wisdom and science are mutually exclusive; on the contrary, one postulates the other. But the fact is that the modern mentality is satisfied with the certainty and the practical utility of its notional and scientific rationalism, neglecting philosophical reasoning (cf. Rom 1:20) and pursuit of truth along the paths of moral uprightness (cf. Jn 3:21); and that makes religious life and the acceptance of faith more difficult.

—Papal audience, January 26, 1972

**What Is Conscience?**  Moral conscience is more exactly the sense, or rather the judgment that one gives to oneself, often spontaneously, with regard to one's way of acting: good (a good conscience), or bad (a bad conscience). This judgment is in itself a reference to the order that must govern our conduct, the use of our freedom, the accomplishment of our duty, the direction and state of our life particularly as regards God.

—Papal audience, March 15, 1972

**The Inner Dialogue of Conscience: Distinguishing between Good and Evil**  Man has the privilege of knowing the order in which he lives; and the first imperative that arises in him, when he discovers this order, is the following; live according to this order; that is, according to your nature; respect your being. This is instinctively expressed in the following mental and operative formula; be good and avoid evil.

The concept of good and evil is at the root of our activity, and arises spontaneously in our conscience. The whole moral system, it can be said, springs from it. Hence the great pedagogical importance of stressing the sense of good and evil, and of developing this sense in an inner dialogue of conscience, which is in fact called moral when it refers to the distinction of what is good from what is evil, and when it is aware that it starts out from the requirement of radical conformity with our rational nature, penetrated in its turn by a transcendent requirement, which is God's creative will.          —Papal audience, July 14, 1972

**The Guidance and Context of Conscience**  A man without a conscience is like a ship without a rudder. That is, without guidance. He lacks the knowledge of the real values of life and the knowledge of his purpose in life. The moralists tell us so when they teach that the goodness of a human action depends on the object to which it is directed, and also on the circumstances in which it is carried out, and on the intention which prompts it.

—Papal audience, August 2, 1972

**Remorse Can Be Positive or Negative**   Remorse is the revenge of conscience; and it can be directed, as actual and literary experience teaches us, toward negative expressions of the spirit, such as anguish or despair (remember the tragic end of Judas, Mt 27:3–5), or toward positive ones (remember the tears that regenerated Peter's love, Mt 26:75; and Jn 21:15–17).

—Papal audience, March 15, 1972

**External Influences on Conscience**   This return to one's own moral conscience is all the more desirable today the more modern education qualifies man for the exercise of thinking and for the autonomous choice of his own decision; and also the more our psychology is pervaded, often almost without our being aware of it, with external stimuli and impressions.

The environment, public opinion, fashion, the incentives of passion, economic interests, innumerable distractions prevent us, in practice, from having recourse to our conscience. Original, personal action is overcome by influences of every kind, so that man lives blindly, almost conditioned and guided by the phenomenalism of the things that surround him and by the compelling and conventional mechanism that sweeps him along.

—Papal audience, August 2, 1972

**Faith: The Church's Greatest Need**   We are asking what the Church needs most today; and we answer: faith. That is, adherence to the Word of God, to divine revelation, which has in Christ its focal point, and in the Church its safekeeping, its testimony, its interpretation.        —Papal audience, October 11, 1972

**Faith and Faithfulness**   What we have said would not be complete if we did not add that from adherence to faith is derived a fundamental moral commitment, a general, primary duty, which is faithfulness. Not for nothing does the believer define himself as a member of the faithful.

Faithfulness is the reason for living; it is not laziness, it is not a chain restraining the boldness of talent and love; but when, as we were saying, it consists in adherence to our "Credo," which never ages and never is exhausted, it opens to them a path in order, always positive, strong and happy.

Faithfulness is derived from faith, which must become the operative principle of the Christian. Let us remember St. Paul's, words, the basis of his doctrine: "the righteous man lives on faith" (Gal 3:11; Heb 10:38; Rom 1:17); he says, mind, on faith, not just with faith.

That is, the righteous man, the real Christian, draws from faith the reason and the norm of his life, and not just by adhering to faith as a mere exterior garb more or less qualifying or decorating his existence.    —Papal audience, October 11, 1972

**Mediocrity Distinguishes Faith**   We would say only this: today either you live your faith with devotion, depth, vigor and joy, or that faith dies out.    —Address to the International Conference on Charismatic Renewal, May 19, 1970

**Discernment: Reading Divine Signs**   In fact there are innumerable events in life and human situations which offer the opportunity for a discreet but incisive statement of what the Lord has to say in this or that particular circumstance. It suffices to have true spiritual sensitivity for reading God's message in events.    —*Evangelii Nuntiandi*, 1975

# *Conclusion*

After the Bible, it would be difficult to think of a text more suited to *lectio divina* than a Catholic creed, particularly one composed by an articulate, dialogical pope in tune with his flock and the modern world.

Paul's poignant, profound, and pithy way of communicating ensures that each line of the creed will contain ample possibilities for reflection and application. We can select one line or several together. We can integrate a line from the creed with another of Paul's messages, either from this or another chapter.

As discussed in the Introduction and elaborated on by Paul, faith is not a static concept. Its expression in action reveals its content and character. Just as faith is a dynamic, lived reality, so is *lectio,* which cannot be confined to quiet time. It cannot be compartmentalized. It needs to flow into the rest of our life and influence and interact with it. The word or central message we receive in *lectio* is meant to be a centering point in our day. We return to it at various times during the day as a way of touching base with God and ourselves and assessing our position and progress.

This is not a mechanical process prone to evoke scrupulosity. The Spirit works in us to call us back to our word, to remind us of the message we have been given. This in itself requires faith and discernment, as rarely does God spell out everything for us.

As with the rest of the Christian life, living our faith through the practice of *lectio* is a joint effort with God and others (e.g., through counsel, dialogue, or shared *lectio*). We have to do our part, using our abilities as best we can. The traditional maxim applies: pray as if everything depends on God; act as if everything depends on you. Paul's human development and spirituality (see the chapters on joy and suffering) insights help us optimize our attitude and efforts.

Paul's message on faith, whether with regards to content, as in his creed, or with respect to belief and practice, can be a centering point for us. The word or message we receive can be an invitation to deeper cooperation and intimacy with God, others, and the Church.

Using the metaphor of a prominent medieval authority on *lectio divina,* the twelfth-century Carthusian monk Guigo II, let us take Paul's words and chew on them like grapes, masticating and ruminating them for all they have to offer, and digesting them in the Spirit and our conscience. Faith, like hope and love, is never in a hurry. Let us take our time on this profound subject, recognizing that the project is God's first and ours second, and entrust our efforts and outcomes to Him.

## Chapter 7

# Hope

*Will the world ever succeed in changing that selfish and bellicose mentality which, up to now, has been interwoven in so much of its history? It is hard to foresee; but it is easy to affirm that it is toward that new history, a peaceful, truly human history, as promised by God to men of good will, that we must resolutely march. The roads thereto are already well marked out for you; and the first is that of disarmament. . . .*

*You work here not only to avert conflicts between states, but also to make them capable of working the ones for the others. You are not satisfied with facilitating mere coexistence between nations: you take a much greater step forward, one deserving of our praise and support — you organize the brotherly collaboration of peoples.*

*In this way a system of solidarity is set up and its lofty civilized aims win the orderly and unanimous support of all the family of peoples for the common good and for the good of each individual.*

*This aspect of the organization of the United Nations is the most beautiful; it is its most truly human visage; it is the ideal of which mankind dreams on its pilgrimage through time; it is the world's greatest hope; it is, we presume to say, the reflection of the loving and transcendent design of God for the progress of the human family on earth — a reflection in which we see the message of the Gospel, which is heavenly become earthly.* —Pope Paul VI, Address to the
U.N. General Assembly, October 4, 1965

Paul VI was a prophet of hope. He was able to be such because he was in touch with reality and the hopeful message of the Bible and the Church, particularly as narrated in the Gospels.

Paul led the Church at a time in which hope itself was tested. Optimists in both the religious and secular realms were confronted with grim realities. In the United States, activists in the peace movement were in tension with political and corporate proponents of the escalation of the Vietnam War.

The Johnson administration sought to establish a "Great Society," only to have it flounder amid social inequality and unrest, inflation, and the war.

The civil rights movement was faced with both official opposition, e.g., Governor Wallace of Alabama, and indirect opposition: even when laws were changed, those entrusted to administer them did not always comply, and interactions and circumstances not directly under the jurisdiction of law (e.g., hiring practices, social relationships) were subject to the same prejudices and discriminations.

The nuclear disarmament movement struggled to make headway against the arms race while tensions grew not only between the United States and the Soviets, but also between the Soviets and their satellite countries (e.g., Czechoslovakia, whose uprising was suppressed by Soviet tanks in 1968). Naive advocates of the sexual revolution sought to spread free love, only to discover that love always comes at a cost and with responsibilities. Pope Paul took office just five months before a man who epitomized hope, President John F. Kennedy, was assassinated.

Within the Church, hope had its ups and downs as well. The Vatican Council began and ended on a hopeful theme. Paul's closing comments, some of which are included in this chapter, were an inspiration to many. The council issued a document entitled "Joy and Hope" (*Gaudium et Spes,* Pastoral Constitution on the Church in the Modern World), which was frequently referenced by both Paul and John Paul II. It articulated the Church's identity and attitude with respect to the modern world and is the most inspiring and accessible of the council documents.

Paul's comments during and after the council were filled with hope, yet always remained rooted in reality. Even after the disappointments that inevitably follow an event of this magnitude, Paul retained his optimism, focusing many of his comments on the Holy Spirit's activity within the Church.

Paradoxically, Paul also addressed evil currents and the demonic within the modern world and the Church, using the term "the smoke of Satan" to identify evil's infiltrations into the Church. With Paul's approval, The Sacred Congregation for the Doctrine of the Faith commissioned a study on the subject "Christian Faith and Demonology," which was published in the July 10, 1975, issue of the Vatican newspaper, *L'Osservatore Romano.*

Paul held on to his hope because it was rooted in the Lord. He did not have naive, overly optimistic expectations of himself, the Church, or the world. To quote his namesake, Paul hoped against hope (cf. Rom 4:18), holding nothing back and abandoning himself to the Lord. Hope, like faith, targets what is unseen. It is an act of trust. Hope enables us to persevere even when feelings and rationality tell us to give up.

Many Catholics' agenda for Church renewal were not fulfilled. Hopes were misplaced, disappointed, and betrayed. St. Augustine commented that two things kill the soul: despair and false hope. How difficult it is to have our dreams dashed, yet it is far from an uncommon occurrence. Some people never recover from traumatic events like disability, divorce, or the loss of a loved one, a business, or a job.

Despite the discouraging evidence and daunting challenge before us, we are called to continue hoping against hope. And what are the consequences of this?

Perseverance, joy, purposefulness, humility, faith, suffering. That's right, the virtues and values profiled in this book. Hope binds these together through the motivation and endurance that it inspires, giving us direction and purpose. St. Paul says that character produces a hope that does not disappoint (cf. Rom 5:4–5) because it is fulfilled by God's love and the Spirit.

Like the Psalms, Paul VI's words help us root our hopes in the Lord rather than in human beings. Freed from naiveté, scrupulosity, and egotism, turning our eyes toward God (cf. Ps 123:1–2; Heb 12:1–2) helps us resist the fantasies, false promises, and blind alleys that the world offers us.

Perhaps even more than during Paul's time, the world and Church need hope. The spread and entrenchment of materialism and hedonism are such that for many persons and institutions agendas and tangible results have become an obsession and idol. There is little reason to hope because everything is focused on present pleasures and future security.

Christian hope is rooted in abandonment to divine providence and subordination of our will and agenda to God's. As with the other theological virtues, faith and love, this requires an ongoing effort of our whole selves (which *lectio* helps facilitate) in communion with fellow believers. We don't reach our goal and destination until the next life, so we're constantly in a state of hope. This keeps us alert and headed in the right direction.

In contrast, the loss of hope leads to stagnancy, depravity, or despair. Because of his compassionate sensitivity to modern persons and problems, Paul sought and offered a remedy to this hopelessness. His words can help us rediscover the purpose, possibilities, and manifestations of hope in our life. In a spirit of hope, let us read on.

# HOPE

**The Church Shares in Humanity's Hopes**   The joys and the hopes, the griefs and anxieties of the men of this age, especially those who are poor or in any way afflicted, these too are the joys and hopes, the griefs and anxieties of the followers of Christ. Indeed, nothing genuinely human fails to raise an echo in their hearts.                                    — *Gaudium et Spes*

**Passionate Hope for Intimacy with God**   No one is ever close enough to God. Those closest to him burn most with the desire to come still closer. As St. Augustine exhorts: "We must search as one who expects to find; and so find as one who would search further."                                              —Epiphany, 1956

**Looking for the Good in Life**   We should be as punctilious in looking for the good in every manifestation of life as we are in searching out defects and deviations. This does not mean glossing things over and making ourselves and others believe that for a human phenomenon to possess one good feature is enough to qualify it as good.

We want to encourage that partial good, make it an aspiration toward a genuine and complete good.... Otherwise we can neither understand our era nor benefit it, nor will we be faithful to the redemptive message of the Word whose disciples and teachers we want to be. —Lent, 1961

**The Fundamental Sin of Despair**  There is a word in religious and Christian language which is very full and rich in meaning, a word which recurs in profane language also, but which rises up here with all the beauty and strength of the sun, and that word is hope.

Keep it always in your hearts, my sons. I should say that there is only one sin you can commit in this place, the sin of despair.
—To the inmates of Regina Coeli, a Roman jail, April 9, 1964

**The Source of Christian Hope**  The Christian's hope comes primarily from the fact that he knows that the Lord is working with us in the world, continuing in his Body which is the Church — and, through the Church, in the whole of mankind — the Redemption which was accomplished on the Cross and which burst forth in victory on the morning of the Resurrection (cf. Mt 28:30; Phil 2:8–11). This hope springs also from the fact that the Christian knows that other men are at work, to undertake actions of justice and peace working for the same ends. For beneath an outward appearance of indifference, in the heart of every man there is a will to live in brotherhood and a thirst for justice and peace, which is to be expanded.
—*Octogesima Adveniens,* 1971

**The Dynamic Nature of Hope**  Hope is the moving force of human dynamism; more than that, as a theological virtue, it is the force which moves Christian dynamism.

This raises the question of making an analysis of hope in the modern mentality, and We will leave you to do that. You

will immediately see that modern man lives by hope. That is
to say, that his soul is tensed toward the future, toward some
good which is to be attained. What he has now does not satisfy
him, but urges him on and torments him to get more, to find
something else.                          —Papal audience, May 27, 1970

**Hope Underlies Action to Improve on the Past**   Study, work,
progress, contestation, and even revolution are so many forms
of hope in action. This rush forward, so characteristic of our
time, is wholly moved by hope. Those who have least liking for
the past and the present give their hearts to the future, that is
to say, they hope.                       —Papal audience, May 27, 1970

**The Hope of Youth**   St. Thomas well says that hope abounds
in the young. But if they are disappointed in their hope of attaining some kind of better thing in the future, they fall into despair.
This often happens in the critical and pessimistic psychology
of so many other people who are also children of our time.
                                          —Papal audience, May 27, 1970

**Hope Contrasted with Desire**   The Christian is the man of
hope, and does not know despair. There is a difference between
the Christian and the modern secular man in regard to hope.
    The latter is a *vir desideriorum,* a man of many desires (there
is a close relation between desire and hope; hope comes under
the instincts of strength, but desire comes rather under the instincts to enjoy; yet both strive toward future goods). The man
of desires seeks to shorten the distance between himself and
the goods to be attained; he is a man of short-term hopes, he
wants to satisfy them soon. Tangible, economic and temporal
hopes are more easily satisfied; they are therefore quickly exhausted, become empty, and often leave the heart disappointed.
His hopes do not ennoble the mind; they do not give life its
full meaning and they turn the course of life along paths of
questionable progress.                   —Papal audience, May 27, 1970

**Authentic Hope Is Rooted in Grace**   But the Christian is the
man of true hope, that which aims at attaining the supreme
good. He knows that in his efforts to attain his desire he has the

help of that same supreme Good which unites with hope the confidence and the grace to fulfill it. —Papal audience, May 27, 1970

**Christian Hope Can Absorb Secular Hope**  Both hopes, secular and Christian, are motivated by deficiencies in our present conditions, by pain, poverty, remorse, need, dissatisfaction. But they are kept by another, different force, and Christian hope can absorb all the truly human and honest tension in secular hope.

Is not this the leading idea in the great pastoral constitution *Gaudium et Spes* published by the recent council? "There is nothing truly human which does not find an echo in the hearts" of Christ's disciples (no. 1, cf. Terence's "Humani nihil a me alienum puto," nothing human is alien to me).

—Papal audience, May 27, 1970

**Hope Underlies Development**  One of the best assured invariable principles of your action is that the finest technical achievements and the greatest economic progress cannot effect by themselves the development of a people. However necessary they may be, planning and money are not enough. Their indispensable contribution, like that of the technology which they sponsor, would be sterile were it not made fruitful by men's confidence and their progressive conviction that they can little by little get away from their miserable condition through work made possible with means at their disposal.

—Conference of the Food and Agriculture Organization,
November 16, 1970

**Christ the Messenger of True Hope**  We would like to have true hope, hope that does not die with the passage of time, hope that guarantees real and total satisfaction to the natural aspirations of the heart; and these are the greater and more demanding in proportion to the culture and advancement of the man of today.

Yes, Christ answers once more, I am the bread of life; he who eats this bread will live forever.

It is the small Child of Bethlehem who is spreading today his silent and irresistible message. Who will listen to it? Who will accept it? —Christmas Message, 1970

**Hope Is Essential to Life**    We notice in humanity a sad need and, in a certain sense, a prophetic need of hope; it is like the need for breath in order to live. Without hope there is no life. Man's activity is more conditioned by the expectation of the future than by the possession of the present.

Man has need of finality, of encouragement, and a foretaste of future joy. Enthusiasm which is the spring of action and of risk cannot originate without a strong and serene hope. Man has need of optimism which is sincere and not deceptive.

—Easter Sunday Message, April 11, 1971

**Our Hope Is Not in Vain**    And so, friends who are listening to us today, we are in a position to give to you a message of hope. Man's cause is not only not lost, it is secure. The great ideas which are the guiding lights of the modern world shall not be put out. The unity of the world shall be achieved. The dignity of the human person shall be recognized not only formally but effectively.

The inviolability of life, from that in the mother's womb to that of old age, shall have general and effective support.

Unworthy social inequalities shall be overcome. Relationships between peoples shall be peaceful, reasonable, and fraternal.

Neither egoism nor arrogance nor indigence nor licentiousness nor ignorance nor the many deficiencies which still characterize and afflict modern society shall impede the establishment of a true human order, a common good and a new civilization.

—Easter Sunday Message, April 11, 1971

**The Secret of Hope Is the Easter Message**    Neither misery nor the loss of goals attained nor sorrow nor sacrifice nor temporal death shall be able to be abolished. But every human misery shall be able to have assistance and comfort; it shall even know that higher value which our secret can confer upon every human weakness.

Hope will not be extinguished because of the inner power of this secret, which in fact is not a secret for anyone who is listening to us today. You understand it: it is the secret of which we speak, it is the Easter message.

—Easter Sunday Message, April 11, 1971

**Hope Is Founded upon Faith**    Every hope is founded upon a certainty, upon a truth which in the human drama is not limited to being experimental and scientific. True hope which must support man's fearless journey in life is founded upon faith. This faith in fact in the language of the Scriptures "is the assurance of things hoped for" (Heb 11:1); in the context of history it is the coming, it is He whom we are celebrating today: the Risen Jesus.

—Easter Sunday Message, April 11, 1971

**The Realism of Christian Hope**    It is not a dream, it is not utopian, it is not a myth; it is the realism of the Gospel. And upon this realism we believers establish our conception of life, of history and of terrestrial civilization itself. Our hope transcends the latter, but at the same time it urges us to its desired and confident conquests.    —Easter Sunday Message, April 11, 1971

**The Hope for God**    There exists in the human spirit a deep aspiration, a mystical wistfulness, a certain predisposition to understand something more about God, a secret hope to reach Him in some way; in the intuition that the slightest drop of this cognitive possession of the living God would fill it with ineffable joy.    —Papal audience, December 22, 1971

**Youth Need Guidance**    We think that we have every reason to have confidence in Christian youth: youth will not fail the Church if within the Church there are enough older people able to understand it, to love it, to guide it and to open up to it a future by passing on to it with complete fidelity the Truth which endures. Then new workers, resolute and fervent, will in their turn enter upon spiritual and apostolic work in the fields which are white and ready for the harvest. Then the sower and the reaper will share the same joy of the kingdom (cf. Jn 4:35–36).

—*Gaudete in Domino*, 1975

**Jesus Fulfills the Spiritual Vacuum of Youth**    It seems to us in fact that the present world crisis, which is marked by a great confusion among many young people, partly betrays a senile and definitely out-of-date aspect of a commercial, hedonistic and materialistic civilization which is still trying to present itself as the gateway to the future. Even in its very excesses, the instinctive reaction of many young people against this illusion takes on a certain importance.

This generation is waiting for something else. Having suddenly been deprived of protective traditions, then bitterly deceived by the vanity and spiritual vacuum of false novelties, atheistic ideologies and certain deleterious forms of mysticism, will not this generation come to discover or rediscover the sure and unalterable newness of the divine mystery revealed in Jesus Christ?

Has not He, in the splendid words of St. Irenaeus, "brought all newness by bringing His own person"?

*—Gaudete in Domino,* 1975

## *Conclusion*

Like faith, hope is a virtue integral to the practice of *lectio divina* because it involves things anticipated but unseen (cf. Rom 8:24–25; 1 Cor 15:19; 2 Cor 4:16–18) and from a human perspective uncertain. Assimilation of *lectio,* Scripture, and Pope Paul VI's teachings do not relieve us of the need to persevere in hope. We can't expect to be continually inspired, enlightened, edified, and instructed. As in marriage, the primary biblical image for our relationship with God, we have to navigate the monotonous flatlands and challenging valleys in order to reach the peaks and our eventual destination.

Hope is an undercurrent of our practice of *lectio* because we are not seeking immediate results or continual stimulation when we interact with God's word or Paul's teachings. To the contrary, we can expect to be challenged, confused, and disturbed as God turns our world and expectations upside down. God's word is designed to make us whole and holy rather than comfortable.

Paul VI's writings indicate that our call and transformation is not to a life of ease and assurance. What Scripture promises must be hoped for and taken on faith. As St. Paul observes: "We walk by faith, not by sight" (2 Cor 5:7). "If for this life only we have hoped in Christ, we are of all people most to be pitied" (1 Cor 15:19).

Pope Paul preached and exemplified hope. His words take the best of the past in the context of the present and point to the future, whence is our hope. *Lectio* is a spiritual and personal growth model driven by faith, hope, love, and other spiritual values rather than earthly values such as results and pleasure. Neither Paul nor *lectio* promises anything other than a reason to hope. In light of the good news of Jesus Christ, that is sufficient.

## Chapter 8

# Love

*If you wish to be brothers, let the arms fall from your hands.
One cannot love while holding offensive arms. Those armaments, especially those terrible arms which modern science
has given you, long before they produce victims and ruins,
nourish bad feelings, create nightmares, distrust, and somber
resolutions; they demand enormous expenditures; they obstruct projects of union and useful collaboration; they falsify
the psychology of peoples.* —Pope Paul VI, Address to the
U.N. General Assembly, October 4, 1965

One of the difficult tasks in compiling the selections in this book was
deciding how to treat Paul's most controversial subject, heterosexual
love. I considered incorporating chastity into this chapter, because
chastity is also charity (which is a traditional Christian synonym for
love), but thought that given chastity's sexual connotations and love's
multiple meanings it was better to treat them separately, though they
obviously overlap.

Paul's teaching on love is hard to define because it touches upon
the whole of Christian life. In an era where love was presented in
superficial, naive, and narcissistic terms, Paul described love in biblical
terms as reflected in his namesake's classic definition in 1 Cor 13 and
in the two great commandments (cf. Mt 22:34–40).

When Paul VI speaks of love, he frequently refers to supporting
texts such as the Bible, Vatican II documents, or the writings of
the saints so that his comments will be grounded in the Christian
tradition.

Paul discusses love in the context of the entire spiritual and apostolic life. He was fond of making connections and pointing out

94

inter-relationships. Reading Paul is like a course in the Christian life and tradition.

Paul candidly acknowledged the demands of Christian life, often prefacing his moral exhortations with "whether we like it or not." He recognized the resistance of the human spirit to the call of the Gospel, and while he was diligent in handing on the faith he was compassionately sensitive to human weakness and limitations. As a disciple of St. Augustine, he had a profound sense of the mercy of God amid human misery.

Paul was not a demonstrative person and did not put on grandiose displays for the purpose of edifying or entertaining crowds or the media. Rather, he carefully selected and delivered meaningful gestures, recognizing that love is often communicated in little things that do not overwhelm.

Similarly, Paul did not wax eloquently on love, choosing instead to offer direct, pithy counsel and exhortations rather than abstract concepts or ponderous platitudes. Let us follow his lead by getting to the subject directly and applying his teachings on love in the practical circumstances of our lives.

## *LOVE*

**Taking Love For Granted** We owe so much to the love and help of others, and we forget so easily! — Holy Week, 1963

**Love of God and Neighbor** We remember only too well that we shall be judged by the real love which we have shown toward our neighbor, especially when he is in need, suffering, cast down (cf. Mt 25:31ff.). In that matter We set no limit.

But we must always remember that the beginning of love of our neighbor is our love of God. He who forgets the reasons why we have to call ourselves the brethren of mankind, namely, the Fatherhood of God which we have in common, could well at a given moment forget the grave burdens attaching to such brotherhood and see in his own likeness no longer a brother, but a stranger, a rival, an enemy.

To give pride of place in religion to humanitarianism leads to the danger of transforming theology into sociology and of forgetting the basic hierarchy of things and their values: "I am the Lord thy God...thou shalt have no other God but me" (cf. Ex 20:1ff.); so it is written in the Old Testament; and in the New Christ teaches us: "Love God...this is the first and greatest commandment. The second is like unto this: thou shalt love thy neighbor as thyself" (Mt 27:37–39).

—Papal audience, July 10, 1968

**Duty's Deeper Name: Love**    It is all a matter of seeing what kind of liberation gives to man his fullness. What is said of the individual person may also be said of human society and its civilization. It must always be developing morally, that is, in a human and Christian sense, and therefore culturally, socially, economically, and so on.

In the last analysis, this means that the real driving force of our existence is duty. For us Christians duty has an even stronger and deeper name: love. Jesus said, "Thou shalt love God with thy whole heart, and thou shalt love thy neighbour as thyself: this is the whole law...." (Mt 22:37–40).

—Papal audience, March 18, 1970

**Love Ignites Our Search for God**    The problem is concerned with the reality of man and things; it is not an ontological but a psychological and pedagogical one. How can God be sought in these conditions? It would be rash to give a reply to a problem of such scope and complexity in words so brief and transient as these. Yet we will point out a way; it is not the only way, or the decisive way, but an indication and a beginning.

We can start by arousing man's desire for true and complete, full and authentic humanism (this is the apostolate of today). That desire contains a connatural way of getting beyond man's one-dimensional, that is, materialist and positive level; it also stirs in him a wakeful *sense* of God, together with interest and hope.

Then, if the Master comes to meet him, that really becomes a search, but more than a search, for it also becomes an initial divine victory and turns into modern man's existential adventure. It will be very fine.

And how can we start it off? With love and charity. Charity is a method: it is truth's preparatory school. That would take too long to explain, but think and pray about it.

—Papal audience, August 26, 1970

**The Two Greatest Commandments**   We prefer to conclude with a consoling response to that rightful desire to have the whole of the moral law summed up in a simple and comprehensive synthesis. That response was given by Christ himself. He was asked what is the first and highest precept of the whole divine law, which was expressed in the Mosaic Law and had developed into all the legal formalism of the time.

You know the answer he gave. It was twofold, and it sums up "all the Law and the Prophets." One part of it is vertical, as we say today, and it is the source of the other, which is horizontal. That law is: Love God and love your neighbor (Mt 22:36 ff.).

This is the synthesis, with all its implications. This is the Gospel. This is life: "Do this and thou shalt live" (Lk 10:28), we conclude with Jesus.          —Papal audience, October 7, 1970

**Love, Humanity's Greatest Potential**   A great deal has been said and written about that mysterious being, man: about the resources of his intellect, capable of penetrating the secrets of the universe and of subjugating material things, utilizing them for his own purposes; about the grandeur of the human spirit, manifested in the admirable works of science and art; about his nobility and his weakness; his triumphs and his wretchedness.

But that which characterizes man, that which is the most intimate element in his being and his personality, is the capacity to love, to love to the end, to give himself with that love that is stronger than death and extends into eternity.

—The Occasion of the Canonization of the
Forty Martyrs of England and Wales, October 25, 1970

**The Witness of Martyrs**    The martyrdom of Christians is the most sublime expression and sign of this love, not only because the martyr remains faithful to his love to the extent of shedding his blood, but also because this sacrifice is performed out of the loftiest and noblest love that can exist, namely, love for Him who created and redeemed us, who loves us as only He can love, and expects from us a response of total and unconditioned donation, that is, a love worthy of our God.

May the Lord grant us the grace that, in the times of growing religious indifferentism and theoretical and practical materialism, the example and intercession of the Forty Holy Martyrs may encourage us in faith and strengthen our authentic love for God, for his Church and for all men.
— The Occasion of the Canonization of the
Forty Martyrs of England and Wales, October 25, 1970

**Liberty Flows from Love and Responsibility**    Liberty is an extremely precious and extremely delicate faculty (cf. 1 Pt 2:16). So that liberty may remain for us that divine reflection which it is, let us seek to protect it, and first of all within ourselves. It is true that conscience must be its guide, but conscience itself must be guided by the science of divine and human things; the truth is liberating.

It is true that liberty must be able to operate without hindrance, but it must be directed toward the good, and this imperative orientation is called a sense of responsibility, it is called duty.

It is true that liberty is a personal prerogative, but it cannot but respect the rights of others. Indeed it cannot be separated from charity, which not only makes us respect the law (cf. Rom 13:1–7) and obedient to the balance of collective coexistence (cf. Col 3:20), but also forbids us the use of licit things if they are harmful to our neighbor (cf. Rom 14:15; 1 Cor 10:23).

It divests us of all selfishness and converts our personal autonomy into an oblation to God (with promises or vows, for example), and into voluntary and generous commitment in the service of others.                    — Papal audience, August 18, 1971

**God Comes First in Christian Morality**   Does a Christian morality exist? That is, an original way of living, which is called
Christian? What is Christian morality? . . .

Our practical conception of life must reserve the first place
for God, religion, faith and spiritual health; and not just an hon-
orary first place, purely formal, or ritual, but also logical and
functional.

My position with regard to God is the most precious and most
important thing. The hierarchy of my duties keeps the first level
for God: "I am the Lord thy God" (Ex 20:2). Christ will repeat it:
"seek first the kingdom of God" (Mt 6:33).

—Papal audience, July 26, 1972

**The Priority of Love of God**   The first orientation of life, the
central axis to which my humanism is geared, remains the
theological one.

The commandment that surpasses and synthesizes all the
others is always the one that bids us love God (cf. Mt 22:37; Dt
9:5). It is a sublime commandment, which is far from easy, but
which in the very effort of its fulfillment produces the motive
and the energy to fulfill the other lower commandments, the
first among which and, in its turn, the sum of the others, is love
of our neighbor, so much so that it is taken as proof of love of
God itself (cf. 1 Jn 2:9; 4:20).

Thus suppression of love of God, in the conviction that love
of our neighbor is sufficient, ( . . . how many people, today, de-
lude themselves that they have simplified the moral problem by
neglecting its fundamental religious principle and reducing it to
a humanistic philanthropy!), also compromises the relationship
of real love for man, a relationship that easily deteriorates, no
longer universal, no longer disinterested, no longer constant. It
may become partial, and therefore a principle of struggle and
hatred.

Far less does the recognition of the religious primacy in
morality produce a selfish and irrational curb on the positive
search for remedies for social ills; on the contrary. Let us recall
the Lord's severe words, "Not every one who says to me, 'Lord,

Lord,' shall enter the kingdom of heaven, but he who does the will of my Father who is in heaven" (Mt 7:21; cf. Mt 25:31–46); and let us recall the Apostle's exhortation: faith working through love (cf. Gal 5:6).                                    —Papal audience, July 26, 1972

**Jesus' Moral Expectations**    Read the Sermon on the Mount, which is, as it were, a synthesis of the Gospel and the program of Christianity. The fact that the Lord brings the essence and perfection of moral life from the outside to within man, to his heart, his thoughts, his conscience, makes this moral life of ours more difficult and grave, particularly if we lack love and grace, which make every commitment, every sacrifice "joyful and ready."

And does not the example of Christ crucified, which He Himself proposed to our imitation, tell us what fortitude, what heroism, can be asked of us Christians? "Anyone who does not take his cross (and He means: mine) and follow in my footsteps is not worthy of me!" (Mt 10:38). You all know the significance these words have had in the history of Christianity and of holiness.                                  —Papal audience, September 6, 1972

**The Moral Demands of the Gospel**    The question rises spontaneously; how is it possible to impose such a serious duty on people of this world? We know only too well their laziness, even their incapacity for great ideals, moral ones particularly, which are not confined to utopian speculation but demand practical and concrete applications in actual life. We know, too, their frailty in consistency of action and their deceptive happiness in yielding to their passions and to the stimulus of interest and pleasure.

Is such a severe interpretation of Christian life correct? Is not the evangelical law indulgent to human weakness? Does it not free us from the burdens of legalism and moralism? What a long answer such a complex and radical question would require! Let us give a very summary answer for the present.

Christian life does, indeed, free us from the weight of norms unnecessary for perfection, which consists substantially in charity (cf. Col 3:14), and which denounces in pharisaism an intolerable hypocrisy (cf. Mt 23).

But it is not lax; on the contrary, it is morally serious and severe; just read the Sermon on the Mount. It aims entirely at a perfection that begins within man and therefore is binding on the direction of freedom from its very first roots, the heart (cf. Mt 15). —Papal audience, November 4, 1972

**Grace Makes the Impossible Possible**    But we must take into account, above all, that the human action of the Christian enjoys a marvelous and incalculable interior aid, grace. Does not the Master say to strengthen the disciples, frightened by the demands of evangelical morality: "With men this is impossible, but with God all things are possible"? (Mt 19:26).

This is a vital point for the follower of Christ and for the whole doctrine and practice of Christian life and perfection, that is, for the conquest of holiness. Grace makes Christ's yoke light and sweet (cf. Mt 11:30). Grace operating in the human spirit multiples its forces, to the extent of making self-sacrifice, poverty, chastity, obedience, the cross, pleasant.

—Papal audience, November 4, 1972

**God's Gift of Himself**    God has revealed himself in love, He has made himself proportionate to our extreme aspirations; God has had a heart for every deficiency, for every wickedness of ours, for every sin of ours. God has offered himself to us as mercy, grace, salvation, as a joyful, glorious surprise (cf. Rom 9:23; Col 1:27; 1 Cor 5:9). —Papal audience, December 20, 1972

# Conclusion

Fr. Luke Dysinger, O.S.B., an international authority on *lectio divina*, aptly entitled his audiocassette program and classic article on *lectio divina* "Accepting the Embrace of God." *Lectio* is a path to intimacy with God and others through giving of the whole self, and thus is a form of lovemaking.

More specifically and practically, what characteristics does *lectio* share with lovemaking? It is unpredictable, natural, fulfilling, and spontaneous while necessitating commitment. It is a form of communication in which we gradually progress to the crescendo of intimacy.

Understanding its background and mechanics can be helpful, though observers and teachers cannot adequately communicate it. There is no substitute for experience. It takes patience, gentleness, and practice to grow in confidence and competence. Each experience is unique, subjective, and personal, yet also subject to objective principles.

In order to love well, whether spiritually, relationally, or intimately, you have to be serious and relaxed, disciplined as well as playful. Being rigid detracts from efforts and experiences.

What's to be rigid about? The main criteria of authenticity is to be yourself and try your best — a tall enough order without any self-inflicted pressure. If that's not enough, you're in the wrong place or relationship. It's always enough with God, who is merciful and understanding, particularly with the vulnerable and humble.

Among modern pontiffs, Paul VI particularly helps us to relax because his teachings are less philosophical, dense, and turgid than John Paul II's, and he constantly qualifies his comments with recognition of human weakness. With all the humiliating experiences he underwent as pope, his teachings projected a humble, down-to-earth disposition that put others at ease and was never condescending or pretentious.

Love is a tough subject to tackle with a direct and challenging source like Paul VI because our failings and vulnerabilities will be exposed amid high standards. To absorb these truths and counsels we need to be properly prepared and disposed.

Lest we become harsh, scrupulous, or bitter, love is the attitude with which we should approach Scripture, life, and the teachings of Paul VI. *Lectio* helps us soak up the nuances and depths of Paul's teachings on love because it is an intimate, subtle, and sensitive process. It helps us process Paul's simultaneously challenging and consoling realism, compassionate forethought, and prudent guidance while opening us to other sources of divine and human nourishment. In this open spirit, let us join Paul in rediscovering how to love.

*Chapter 9*

# Chastity

*You proclaim here the fundamental rights and duties of man, his dignity, his freedom — and above all his religious freedom. We feel that you thus interpret the highest sphere of human wisdom and, we might add, its sacred character. For you deal here above all with human life; and the life of man is sacred; no one may dare offend it.*

*Respect for life, even with regard to the problem of birth, must find here in your assembly its highest affirmation and its most reasoned defense. You must strive to multiply bread so that it suffices for the tables of mankind, and not rather favor an artificial control of birth, which would be irrational, in order to diminish the number of guests at the banquet of life.*

—Pope Paul VI, Address to the
U.N. General Assembly, October 4, 1965

Let's begin by defining chastity. First, we must recognize that it is a positive virtue. Its synonym is sexual purity. Chastity is not designed to withhold sexual pleasure but to direct it to its proper context and ends so as to safeguard the dignity of all involved and fulfill God's purpose. Thus we should begin this chapter with a positive expectation, recognizing that we are going to reflect on a beneficial subject that reveals how something beautiful (sex and personal and relationship integrity) can stay that way and exceed our expectations on a realistic rather than fantasy level.

Pope Paul's teachings on sexuality and marriage were far more than a matter of do's and don'ts. The media and superficial observers focused on prohibitions and isolated arguments, but Paul was concerned about the integrity and well-being of the couple, family, Church, and society.

The defining moment of Paul VI's papacy was his issuance of the encyclical *Humanae Vitae* ("On Human Life") on July 25, 1968. The negative outcry, dissent, and lack of support were so great that for the remaining decade of his pontificate he did not issue another encyclical. Cast as "the birth control encyclical" by the media, it was much more than that. It was a positive statement of marital love in the context of the natural and divine law.

Almost forty years later, *Humanae Vitae* is widely regarded as prophetic for its identification of the connection between contraception and other reproductive and dignity of life issues and the slippery slope to promiscuity, disrespect for the woman and femininity, and marital, family, and societal breakdowns that a relaxing of moral standards would entail.

Understanding the circumstances of this encyclical sheds much light on Paul VI and his pontificate. The first point to recognize is that persons who criticize the encyclical vehemently have likely read it little if at all. It's not the kind of text one can go through in a short time. Few persons of a secular perspective, particularly in the media, are interested enough to give it a fair and thorough read. Most Catholics have not devoted time and effort to understand it, and it has not been communicated lucidly at the pastoral level. Many reactions to it are born primarily of negative experiences, confusion, predispositions, cultural conditioning, agendas, and ignorance rather than enlightened reflection and discernment. All this helps explain John Paul's efforts to affirm and elaborate on it.

Second, reading the encyclical itself is insufficient for understanding Paul's intentions. You have to consider his prior actions (as discussed above) and subsequent comments. The first general audience following the encyclical's publication provided the opportunity to share his concerns and the burden and hopes he carried. Excerpts from this audience are presented in this chapter.

Third, one has to understand the modern history of the birth control issue. First, until the 1930s, most Christian denominations rejected contraception. At the Lambeth Conference in 1930, the

Anglicans reluctantly allowed contraception when used with "right intentions," and other Protestant denominations soon followed suit. In response, Pius XI issued an encyclical, *Casti Connubii,* on December 31, 1930, which upheld the traditional prohibition. Catholicism was not imposing an unprecedented moral requirement.

Pius XII had been the last pontiff to speak in detail on the subject, doing so in an address to Italian midwives on October 29, 1951. His comments have been analyzed and assimilated primarily by theologians, bishops, clergy, and theology students, but rarely by the person in the pew. Further restricting exposure of the address is its limited availability in print. It is found primarily in compendiums of papal teachings on the subject such as *Love and Sexuality* (Consortium Books, 1978).

John XXIII affirmed the traditional prohibition of contraception without expanding upon it, and authorized a multidisciplinary commission to study the question concurrent with Vatican II.

Paul VI inherited this commission along with the expectation that the subject might be addressed in one of the conciliar documents, which turned out to be *Gaudium et Spes,* the Pastoral Constitution on the Church in the Modern World.

Here Paul made two significant decisions. He withdrew the matter from consideration by the council fathers and reserved the decision to himself while allowing the commission to continue its investigations. When the majority decision of the commission recommended limited and discerning use of contraception in specific situations, he engaged in further deliberations. Paul's decision was not made in a vacuum, but in an atmosphere of debate, anticipation, and expectation.

While Paul rejected the commission's recommendation, his encyclical echoed many of its concerns and insights. A careful reading of the encyclical reveals its measured approach and pastoral character. The third and concluding section is filled with pastoral directives and encouraging and consoling comments. The media ignored the cohesiveness, subtleties, and pastoral qualifications of the encyclical, expediently concentrating on Paul's rejection of the commission's recommendation and affirmation of the traditional prohibition.

Bishops' conferences throughout the world issued explanatory statements varying from clarifying and supportive to apologetic and hedging. The two most frequent popular observations on the document were its lack of infallible status and the primacy of an informed conscience. According to these qualifications, married couples had some leeway in their implementation of the teachings, though the official position was that God's mercy, the Church's compassion and support, and confession were the primary recourse for persons unable to comply with the teaching.

In several places in the encyclical Paul acknowledged the difficulties associated with fidelity to his conclusions. He advocated compassion, patience, and understanding toward and on the part of married couples unable to conform to the prohibition, and urged confessors to exercise prudence, discretion, and charity without departing from or minimizing the moral and spiritual principles involved. It remained a dialogue rather than a dictum.

Paul carefully framed his decision in its historical and cultural context. He acknowledged biological, technological, economic, and moral considerations and explicitly left the subject open for further reflection.

In response to John Paul II's subsequent affirmation and strengthening of the prohibition, many commentators and popularizers cite *Humanae Vitae* without mentioning Paul's nuanced comments and pastoral counsel. The result has been a moralistic treatment of the subject stripped of Paul's contextualizing and qualifying commentary. Pastoral, communal, medical, and socioeconomic considerations mentioned by Paul have been marginalized, thereby reducing the subject to a narrow moral and ascetical challenge rather than a joint vocation, supported by the Christian community at large, to fulfill the dual purposes of marital love: procreative (cf. Gen 1:28) and unitive (cf. Gen 2:18–25).

Far from a watering down of Paul's teaching, an informed, contextual understanding requires a fuller intellectual, emotional, and spiritual commitment that while quite challenging to couples also proves to be profoundly beneficial to their growth and well-being.

If this discussion has been surprising, it is likely that the next disclosure will be even more so. As insightful, instructive, and prophetic as Paul's teachings in *Humanae Vitae* and accompanying addresses have proven to be, his lengthy May 4, 1970, address to the Teams of Our Lady in Rome on the occasion of their twenty-fifth anniversary conference actually surpasses the encyclical in pastoral applications and marital insights.

This is not surprising when one considers the pastoral context and accompanying freedom of such an address. A general or private audience carries expectations of considerably less circulation and authoritative significance than an encyclical, resulting in a relaxation of the language and a narrower scope. When Paul speaks to the Teams of our Lady, he presumes their fidelity to Church teaching while at the same time recognizing the difficulties they encounter. Not having to incorporate precise doctrinal language and multiple considerations for a broad audience, he is free to reflect on the vocation of Christian marriage in a direct, down-to-earth fashion.

My initial exposure to this overlooked gem was in a 1974 Liturgical Press publication entitled *Good News for Married Love,* which supplemented *Humanae Vitae* and was accompanied by a lucid introduction.

A treasure of a decidedly different nature is Paul's February 9, 1976, address to the Roman Rota (the Church's highest marital tribunal). Here the pope, who decentralized and liberalized annulment proceedings in light of modern psychological and sociological considerations germane to the spiritual and moral principles involved, affirms these principles in an unequivocal manner, emphasizing the core canonical principle that consent constitutes a marriage.

After the popular impression that money buys annulments, the second most common misconception about annulments is that postmarital behavior is determinative of the validity of the marriage. The crux of the issue is the efficacy of the consents given, a matter that Paul addresses here.

In this annual address, Paul provides guidance to tribunal judges on remaining faithful to the fundamental principles of marriage in their rulings without ignoring pastoral concerns and the mitigating circumstances of modern life.

While sensitive to the subjective considerations involved, Paul exposes the misunderstandings and distortions characteristic not only of secular society but also pastoral and familial settings within the Church. Paul also touches upon the role of marital love and distinguishes it from popular notions more akin to infatuation (which Paul in his eloquence terms "initial amorous passion").

This casuistic address (concerned with the proper application of canon law and marital doctrine and discipline) provides an excellent complement to Paul's pastoral address to the Teams of Our Lady and the authoritative encyclical. Generous excerpts from these combined with Paul's comments both before and throughout his papacy provide a well-rounded portrait of his teachings.

As is typically the case with Paul, a sufficient comprehension and application of his teachings is achieved only when his various comments are contextualized and maintained in a healthy tension, thereby preserving the balance, moderation, and prudence characteristic of his person and papacy and Catholic teachings in general.

Far from a scrupulous, dogmatic portrayal of Catholic sexual morality, Paul's teachings constitute an invitation to respond to the vocation of procreation and conjugal love and unity in a responsible and hopeful manner, confident of divine help in the midst of human weakness. He provides encouragement, guidance, and consolation to support us in our efforts.

## *CHASTITY*

**Polarities of Love: Selfishness and Sacrifice**   The two opposite poles of love are selfishness and sacrifice. The tendency of the first is to extinguish life; of the second to give it....

The marriage union has its basic paradigm in the love of Christ, who sacrificed himself for humanity, redeemed it, and made his Church for this supreme purpose (cf. Eph 5:25). When love leaves this supernatural path it deviates toward a sterile and cruel fear of new life.                          —Holy Week, 1960

**Replacing Lust with Love**   Lust is very near the surface of the flesh; and it is deep in each human being, close to the origin of life, to men's fullness and happiness, to love. It seems almost impossible to restore integrity to the enjoyment of feelings and senses. But this is just what we must do first of all. Human love must be given back the sublime dignity which it only has at its peak, that is when it unfolds according to a higher, exclusive design, the divine design. — Holy Week, 1960

**The Thin Line between Vice and Virtue**   These two aspects should be pointed out to those preparing for married life. On the one side, the ease and danger, the almost fatal degradation of sexual life when not part of the divine design; and on the other its real and ideal beauty if part of God's established order. We must show the young what is involved in choosing between these two. They are like people walking on heights, in danger of catastrophic falls on one side and on the other the bracing joy of reaching the peak. Vice and virtue stand very close to each other. — Holy Week, 1960

**We Need Purity**   We must boldly affirm the need for purity, and that it is both possible and useful. This is not utopian. It is all part of a moral training, the power of which is still acknowledged by many splendid young people who exercise self-domination and respect for others, whose secret is the help of divine grace. Christian education needs revitalizing, refortifying, perfecting on this subject.   — Holy Week, 1960

**The Purpose of Marriage**   Marriage is not a whim, a momentary venture. It is the conscious and definite choice of a state of life which those who enter it consider best, a state created by both the man and the woman not only to compel each other physically but to carry out a design of Providence that determines the human and supernatural destiny of each of them. . . .

If marriage is conceived in this way it fuses in a single emotion, a single purpose, the two greatest voluntary acts of which the human spirit is capable: love and duty. Love follows its rightful path, that of giving itself, pledging itself, utterly and for ever; duty reacquires its energy and force. Such is life when presented and transfigured in Christ. — Holy Week, 1960

**Christ's Model of Sacrificial Love**   Christ's "husbandly" love of the Church is the model which the sacrament of matrimony reproduces as grace in husband and wife, giving them the capacity of turning their family life into virtue lived....

Christ's generous and heroic gift of himself, his sacrificial love, is the epitome of that love — as it is of his love for mankind whom he longed to save, i.e., the Church. Christian love finds its true colors in this sacrificial light.

That is to say, its true fruitfulness depends on the degree to which the rule, synthesized and expressed in all Christianity, is accepted: "He who finds his life will lose it, and he who loses his life for my sake will find it" (Mt 10:39).          —Holy Week, 1960

**From Natural to Christian Love**   So we should study how natural love becomes Christian love. Not only in matters of morality does the grace of the sacrament leave its impress on natural love, though this is already a great step forward, since it causes natural love to develop according to its own sense of integrity and fitness, detracting nothing but bringing out all its intrinsic value; but it does so too by making it holy and, more than anything else, by purifying it. It is a great thing to purify love! Grace, if not resisted, leads to this.

The various components of natural love: instinct, imagination, sensibility, passion, sensuality, rationality, are ordered and governed by an innate spirituality which unifies them and raises them to the supernatural. Natural love, prone to so many corruptions, is ennobled and becomes a channel of grace, which so pervades and informs it that it takes on the image of the greatest love there has ever been, the love of Jesus Christ for his Church.                                        —Holy Week, 1960

**Sustaining Marital Love**   It requires a sustained effort for natural love to yield to the demands of Christian love. Pronouncing the marriage vow is not enough; it must be renewed every day; and particularly on important family occasions such as the birth of a child, an anniversary, or a trial, it must be able to do battle over and over again against the temptations of skepticism, or resigned disappointment, weariness, or self-withdrawal and selfishness that usually come after some years of marriage.

—Holy Week, 1960

**St. Paul's Laws of Marriage**   We know the laws of marriage which St. Paul, echoing Christ, proclaimed; the unity and indissolubility of the marriage vow were firmly taught by him (1 Cor 1:7; 4:10; 4:39–40; Eph 5:31). He tells of the integrity (1 Cor 7:28; 1 Tm 5:14) and dignity (Eph 5:15) of marriage; he reveals its sacramental character and mysterious supernatural depth: 'This is a great mystery' (Eph 5:32). He teaches its sanctifying power (1 Cor 7:14) and he speaks of the virtues which should adorn the family (1 Cor 7:5; Eph 5:28, 33; 1 Tm 3:11), of the values of maternity (1 Tm 5:3ff.; 1 Cor 7:40) and virginity exalted (1 Cor 7:25ff.).                              —Holy Week, 1960

**Vocations and Potentialities within the Family**   A man who really carries out his duties as a father can rise to great heights of manly virtue. And how much each and every member of his family can learn from his kind, authoritative care for them.

And a woman who is a mother in the full sense of that word can achieve such perfection, can be a source of tender virtue and compassion, of true unity for her husband, her children, and the whole of her family!

Children themselves learn goodness in the school of a good family, and can sometimes even improve their parents when their simple innocence awakens in them the image of those angels who watch over them and who gaze on the face of God.

—Holy Week, 1960

**Family Life as a School of Perfection**   This serene and rosy vision of family life should not let us forget its inherent difficulties. As time passes temperaments show their prosaic reality and their defects, provoke irritation which can turn into quarrels, and from quarrels into discord. But we insist in our optimism, remembering that family life is not perfection achieved, but a school of perfection to be achieved.        —Holy Week, 1960

**Forgiveness in Marriage**    From the outset husband and wife must each become adept at improving the other, correcting the other lovingly, being patient, understanding, encouraging. They, more than anyone else, can practice that wonderful love called forgiveness. They can feel its regenerating effect, sometimes dramatically, when the family may seem on the brink of ruin.

*—Holy Week,* 1960

**Celibate Love**    We readily grant that the natural and lawful desire a man has to love a woman and to raise a family is renounced by the celibate in sacred orders; but it cannot be said that marriage and the family are the only way for fully developing the human person. In the priest's heart love is by no means extinct. His charity is drawn from the purest source, (cf. 1 Jn 4:8–16) practiced in the imitation of God and Christ, and is no less demanding and real than any other genuine love (cf. 1 Jn 3:16–18). It gives the priest a limitless horizon, deepens and gives breadth to his sense of responsibility—a mark of mature personality — and inculcates in him, as a sign of a higher and greater fatherhood, a generosity and refinement of heart (see 1 Thes 2:11; 1 Cor 4:15; 2 Cor 6:13; Gal 4:19; 1 Tm 5:1–2) which offer a superlative enrichment.         *—Sacerdotalis Caelibatus,* 1967

**Jesus' Elevation of Marriage**    Matrimony, according to the will of God, continues the work of the first creation (Gen 2:18); and considered within the total plan of salvation, it even acquired a new meaning and a new value. Jesus, in fact, has restored its original dignity (Mt 19:3–8), has honored it (Jn 2:1–11) and has raised it to the dignity of a sacrament and of a mysterious symbol of His own union with the Church (Eph 5:32).

Thus, Christian couples walk together toward their heavenly fatherland in the exercise of mutual love, in the fulfillment of their particular obligations, and in striving for the sanctity proper to them.         *—Sacerdotalis Caelibatus,* 1967

**The Vocation of Celibacy**    But Christ, "Mediator of a superior covenant" (Heb 8:6), has also opened a new way, in which the human creature adheres wholly and directly to the Lord, and is concerned only with Him and with His affairs (see 1 Cor 7:33–35); thus, he manifests in a clearer and more complete way the profoundly transforming reality of the New Testament.

*—Sacerdotalis Caelibatus,* 1967

**Mutual Perfection in Marriage through Union and Procreation**
As a consequence, husband and wife, through that mutual gift of themselves, which is specific and exclusive to them alone, develop that union of two persons in which they perfect one another, cooperating with God in the generation and rearing of new lives.

Married love is before everything else a love distinctly human, that is, of the senses and of the spirit.... It is a matter of a movement of free will, striving, through the joys and sorrows of daily life, for this love not only to endure but, beyond this, to increase, so much so that husband and wife become, as it were, one heart and one spirit, and reach their human perfection together.

*—Humanae Vitae,* 1968

**The Moral Order of Intercourse**  Men rightly observe that a conjugal act imposed on one's partner without regard to his or her condition or personal and reasonable wishes in the matter, is no true act of love, and therefore offends the moral order in its particular application to the intimate relationship of husband and wife.

If they further reflect, they must also recognize that an act of mutual love which impairs the capacity to transmit life which God the Creator, through specific laws, has built into it, frustrates His design which constitutes the norm of marriage, and contradicts the will of the Author of life. Hence to use this divine gift while depriving it, even if only partially, of its meaning and purpose, is equally repugnant to the nature of man and of woman, and is consequently in opposition to the plan of God and His holy will.        *—Humanae Vitae,* 1968

**Side Effects of Therapeutic Means Do Not Make Them Illicit**
On the other hand, the Church does not consider at all illicit

the use of those therapeutic means necessary to cure bodily diseases, even if a foreseeable impediment to procreation should result there from — provided such impediment is not directly intended for any motive whatsoever.          —*Humanae Vitae,* 1968

**Ministers Not Masters of the Source of Life**    But to experience the gift of married love while respecting the laws of conception is to acknowledge that one is not the master of the sources of life but rather the minister of the design established by the Creator.

Just as man does not have unlimited dominion over his body in general, so also, and with more particular reason, he has no such dominion over his specifically sexual faculties, for these are concerned by their very nature with the generation of life, of which God is the source. "Human life is sacred — all men must recognize that fact," Our predecessor Pope John XXIII recalled. "From its very inception it reveals the creating hand of God."

—*Humanae Vitae,* 1968

**Acknowledgment of Difficulties**    Our words would not be an adequate expression of the thought and solicitude of the Church, Mother and Teacher of all peoples, if, after having recalled men to the observance and respect of the divine law regarding matrimony, they did not also support mankind in the honest regulation of birth amid the difficult conditions which today afflict families and peoples.

The Church, in fact, cannot act differently toward men than did the Redeemer. She knows their weaknesses, she has compassion on the multitude, she welcomes sinners. But at the same time she cannot do otherwise than teach the law. For it is in fact the law of human life restored to its native truth and guided by the Spirit of God (see Rom 8). . . .

We have no wish at all to pass over in silence the difficulties, at times very great, which beset the lives of Christian married couples. For them, as indeed for every one of us, "the gate is narrow and the way is hard, that leads to life"(Mt 7:14; see Heb 12:11).

Nevertheless it is precisely the hope of that life which, like a brightly burning torch, lights up their journey, as, strong in spirit, they strive to live "sober, upright and godly lives in this world" (see Tit 2:12), knowing for sure that "the form of this world is passing away" (see 1 Cor 7:31).     *—Humanae Vitae,* 1968

**Recourse to Sacramental Remedies**    Then let them implore the help of God with unremitting prayer and, most of all, let them draw grace and charity from that unfailing fount which is the Eucharist. If, however, sin still exercises its hold over them, they are not to lose heart. Rather must they, humble and persevering, have recourse to the mercy of God, abundantly bestowed in the Sacrament of Penance.

In this way, for sure, they will be able to reach that perfection of married life which the Apostle sets out in these words: "Husbands, love your wives, as Christ loved the Church. . . . Even so husbands should love their wives as their own bodies. He who loves his wife loves himself. For no man ever hates his own flesh, but nourishes and cherishes it, as Christ does the Church. . . . This is a great mystery, and I mean in reference to Christ and the Church; however, let each one of you love his wife as himself, and let the wife see that she respects her husband" (Eph 5:25, 28–29, 32–33).     *—Humanae Vitae,* 1968

**Priestly Compassion toward Couples**    Now it is an outstanding manifestation of charity toward souls to omit nothing from the saving doctrine of Christ; but this must always be joined with tolerance and charity, as Christ Himself showed in His conversations and dealings with men. For when He came, not to judge, but to save the world (see Jn 3:17), was He not bitterly severe toward sin, but patient and abounding in mercy toward sinners?

Husbands and wives, therefore, when deeply distressed by reason of the difficulties of their life, must find stamped in the heart and voice of their priest the likeness of the voice and the love of our Redeemer.

So speak with full confidence, beloved sons, convinced that while the Holy Spirit of God is present to the magisterium proclaiming sound doctrine, He also illumines from within the hearts of the faithful and invites their assent. Teach married couples the necessary way of prayer and prepare them to approach more often with great faith the Sacraments of the Eucharist and of Penance. Let them never lose heart because of their weakness.                                            —*Humanae Vitae*, 1968

***Humanae Vitae* Is Not the Final Word on the Subject**   It clarifies a fundamental chapter in the personal, married, family and social life of man, but it is not a complete treatment regarding man in this sphere of marriage, of the family and of moral probity. This is an immense field to which the Magisterium of the Church could and perhaps should return with a fuller, more organic and more synthetic exposition.

—Papal audience, July 31, 1968

**The Overwhelming Nature of the Contraception Question**
How often have We felt almost overwhelmed by this mass of documentation! How many times, humanly speaking, have We felt the inadequacy of Our poor person to cope with the formidable apostolic obligation of having to make a pronouncement on this matter!

How many times have We trembled before the alternatives of an easy condescension to current opinions, or of a decision that modern society would find difficult to accept, or that might be arbitrarily too burdensome for married life!

—Papal audience, July 31, 1968

**The Church Respects Sexual Love**   All too often the Church has seemed to question human love, but this impression is erroneous. And so today we want to tell you plainly: "No, God is not the enemy of the great realities of human life, and the Church does not in the least underestimate the values which underlie the everyday lives of millions of couples."

—Address to Teams of Our Lady, May 4, 1970

**The Incarnation Elevates Potentialities**   The mystery in which married love is rooted and which throws light on all forms of its expression is the mystery of the Incarnation, which elevates our human potentialities by penetrating them from within.

Far from despising these potentialities, Christian love raises them to their highest level with patience, generosity, strength, and tenderness, as St. Francis de Sales liked to emphasize in praising the married life of St. Louis.

— Address to Teams of Our Lady, May 4, 1970

**The Duality of the Sexes**   Psychological analyses, psychoanalytical studies, sociological surveys, philosophical reflections will certainly be able to shed light on human sexuality and love; but they would blind us if they neglected this fundamental teaching given to us from the beginning: the duality of the sexes was willed by God so that man and woman together might be the image of God, and like Him, a source of life.

— Address to Teams of Our Lady, May 4, 1970

**The Distinctive Union of Husband and Wife**   The union of man and woman differs radically, in fact, from every other form of human relationship. It constitutes a unique reality, namely, the couple, founded on the mutual giving of self to the other: "and they become but one flesh."

— Address to Teams of Our Lady, May 4, 1970

**Intercourse as Communication**   Sexual intercourse is as much a means of expression between husband and wife as it is a means for them to know each other. Intercourse supports and strengthens their love, and then in the fruitfulness of this act the couple finds total fulfillment: in the image of God, the couple becomes a source of life.

— Address to Teams of Our Lady, May 4, 1970

**The Mysterious Marital Transformation**   Two Christians wish to marry; St. Paul forewarns them: "You are no longer your own." They are members of Christ, both of them, "in the Lord." Their union, too, is made "in the Lord," like that of the Church. And this is why their union is a "great mystery. . . . "

— Address to Teams of Our Lady, May 4, 1970

**Drawing Strength from God**   For Christian spouses, the very manifestations of their tenderness are permeated with this love that they draw from the Heart of God. And if the human source of love were in danger of drying up, its divine source is as inexhaustible as the fathomless depths of God's tenderness.

—Address to Teams of Our Lady, May 4, 1970

**Don't Be Discouraged by Failures**   And do not be discouraged by your failures. Our God is a very gentle and good Father, deeply concerned about His children who may find it hard to keep going, and overflowing with love for them.

—Address to Teams of Our Lady, May 4, 1970

**Chastity Is Achieved Little by Little**   Who would not admit that it is only little by little that a human being succeeds in establishing priorities, putting together many tendencies so as to arrange them harmoniously in that virtue of marital chastity wherein the couple find their full human and Christian fulfillment.                     —Address to Teams of Our Lady, May 4, 1970

**Marriage Has Its Stages and Painful Periods**   The journey undertaken by married couples, like every human life, has many stages and includes difficult and painful periods. You experience them over the years.       —Address to Teams of Our Lady, May 4, 1970

**The Paschal Dimension of Marriage**   And "with fear and trembling," but also with wonder and joy, husband and wife discover that in their marriage, as in the union of Christ and the Church, the Easter mystery of death and resurrection is being accomplished.

This does not all mean that husbands and wives are shielded against all failures: "Let him who prides himself on standing take care lest he fall" (1 Cor 10:12). They are not freed from the need of persevering effort, sometimes in cruel circumstances that can only be endured by the realization that they are participating in Christ's passion.

But at least they know that the moral demands of married life, which the Church recalls to them, are not intolerable and impracticable laws but a gift of God to help them attain, by means of and beyond their own weaknesses, the riches of a fully human and Christian love.

— Address to Teams of Our Lady, May 4, 1970

**Human Love Reflects God's Love**   A man and a woman who love each other, the smile of a child, peace in a home are a sermon without words, but an astonishingly persuasive one. In it everyone can already glimpse quite clearly the reflection of another love, a love infinitely attractive.

— Address to Teams of Our Lady, May 4, 1970

**The Passions**   It [the flesh] presents itself as a congenital and environmental tendency as a characteristic attraction of this world. "Do not love the world or the things in the world — writes the apostle St. John in his first letter — if any one loves the world, love for the Father is not in him. For all that is in the world, the lust of the flesh and the lust of the eyes and the pride of life, is not of the Father but is of the world" (1 Jn 2:15–16). These are the three strands of temptation, which lead man's steps away from God. They are usually called passions (cf. James 1:14).                     — Papal audience, March 31, 1971

**Inner and External Stimuli of Temptation**   We are now concerned with the first temptation, which is very strong today, that of the flesh. Because, if every temptation springs from two stimuli, one inner, the other external, we must note that the inner stimulus becomes more urgent if it is not moderated by a precise effort of will, with the development of personal psychology. And the external stimulus, the environmental one, has become more insistent, alluring, exciting, aggressive than ever.

Think of the licentious and pornographic press, diffused with all the tricks of publicity and commerce. Think of the equivocal and worldly appeal of entertainment, of the licentious amusements, of certain private and public morals freed from moderating norms, of the tendencies that are spreading as a result of the so-called permissive "morality" (or immorality), and which allow every baseness and depravation. The environment, if one does not try to immunize oneself with pondered resolution, offers everywhere solicitations to the frailty of the "flesh," especially in the case of the young and inexperienced.

—Papal audience, March 31, 1971

**Temptations of the Flesh Can Be Overcome**    But let it suffice for us, here, to propose once more to your reflection, with
regard to this temptation — which is "legion" (cf. Mk 5:9) —
that is, extremely varied and insistent, two affirmations and a
recommendation. The first affirmation is that victory over the
temptation of the flesh is possible. It is the common conviction,
which finds support and complicity in the very nature of this
temptation, that it is impossible to overcome it, that chastity
is a Utopia, that the experience of its sway over our spirit,
over our moral equilibrium, honest and pure, is tolerable, in
fact instructive, perhaps.

This is not so, beloved brothers and sons! If we wish, we can
keep our body and our spirit chaste. The Master, who speaks
out with extreme severity in this matter (cf. Mt 5:28), does
not propose an impossible thing. We Christians, regenerated by
baptism, though we are not freed from this kind of human weakness, are given the grace of overcoming it with relative facility;
the Spirit can be operative in us with regard to self-control,
continence, chastity (Gal 5:23; Phil 2:3; etc.).

—Papal audience, March 31, 1971

**Purity Flows from Love**    The second affirmation is as follows;
it is a very fine thing to be pure. It is not a burden, it is a
liberation; it is not an inferiority complex, it is an elegance, a
fortitude of the spirit, it is not a source of anxiety and scruples,
it is a maturity of judgement and self-control; it is not ignorance
of the reality of life, it is knowledge disinfected of all possible
contagion, more lucid and penetrating than that opacity typical
of passion and animal experience, it will certainly be innocent,
perhaps ignorant of the pathological phenomenology of corrupt
life, but well aware of the deep realities of good and evil, to
which man is a candidate; it will be so clear-sighted, in fact, as
to detect at the bottom of sinful baseness the possible resources
of repentance and rehabilitation.

Purity is the condition adapted to love, real love, both natural love and the superhuman love dedicated solely to the kingdom of heaven. —Papal audience, March 31, 1971

**Moral Ecology**   And the recommendation follows by itself; we say it to the Father in the usual prayer: "lead us not into temptation"! Let us apply it to ourselves, as if to grant this supreme prayer. We must defend ourselves from the tyrannical temptation of the flesh, if we wish to live the paschal mystery. Inwardly and outwardly; in our hearts, above all, from which come the good and the evil of which we are capable (cf. Mt 15:19; 2 Tm 2:22); and in our surroundings.

Today men are concerned with ecology, that is purification of the physical environment in which man's life takes place. Why should we not be concerned, too, with a moral ecology in which man lives as a man and as a son of God?
—Papal audience, March 31, 1971

**The False Liberation of Undisciplined Sensuality**   The dignity of man! We do not intend now to dwell on this vast subject. It would lead us to deplore bitterly the widely spreading offenses with which so many uncritical forms of modern life degrade man's dignity, particularly with immodest fashions, plays and films which are frivolous or based on passion, immorality of behavior, the perfidious spreading of pornography, the anaesthesia of moral conscience for the sake of sensual consciousness, and the provocative deformation of a wholesome and prudent sex education. Licentious experiences are admitted and encouraged as if they were liberating conquests; liberating from what?

From awareness of good and evil, from respect for the human person, esteem for the truest and most precious values that maintain and enhance the balance between the spirit and the flesh, with modesty, innocence, self-control, with the conscious and generous choice of the truth of love and of its most noble human aims. —Papal audience, July 28, 1971

**Purity Is the Context of Love**    Purity is the atmosphere in
which love breathes.    —Papal audience, September 13, 1972

**Chastity Defiled**    A delicate theme, because it is of an impressive nature, and therefore traditionally treated with great
reticence. Today it is presented with studied and often provok-
ing ostentation.

On the scientific plane, psychoanalysis; on the pedagogical
plane, sexual education; on the literary plane, obligatory eroti-
cism; on the plane of advertising, base allurement; on the plane
of entertainment, indecent exhibition, straining toward the ob-
scene; on the plane of publications, pornographic magazines
spread perfidiously; on the plane of amusements, the pursuit
of the most ignoble and seductive ones; on the plane of love,
which is the highest plane, confusion between sensual and physical selfishness and the lyrical and generous dream of the gift of
oneself.

We must realize that we are living in times when human
animality is degenerating into unrestrained corruption; we are
walking in mud.    —Papal audience, September 13, 1972

**The Subjectivity of Love**    And here there arises a formidable
question: do we really know what love is? Is not this word
among the ones most used, and therefore most difficult to define? Among the words that are polyvalent, in the meanings
attributed to it? Is it not among the most ambiguous words,
even among the most sublimated and the most degraded?

Does it not refer to contradictory forms of our spirit, referred, on the vertical plane, to ascensions toward God, who
is Love and toward whom our natural and supernatural vocation is essentially directed? (St. Augustine's synthesis: Thou, oh
God, made us for Thee; and our heart is restless until it rests
in Thee! *Conf.* 1, 1); and referred — this same word — to the
most vulgar and degrading descents of sensual and even unnatural animality, does it not drag people down, like the inevitable
pull of gravity, below the levels of all decency and all honest
happiness?

And on the horizontal that is the interpersonal place, cannot love mean now the most generous dedication, now the most selfish lust, or even both at the same time? It will not be easy to give a univocal meaning to the ambiguous word "love," which fluctuates between "eros" and "agape" (charity), between instinctive passionate sympathy and the aspiration to good, to happiness, to life. — Papal audience, September 20, 1972

**Family Observance of Liturgy of the Hours**   In accordance with the directives of the council the Institutio Generalis de Liturgia Horarum rightly numbers the family among the groups in which the Divine Office can suitably be celebrated in community.... No avenue should be left unexplored to ensure that this clear and practical recommendation finds within Christian families growing and joyful acceptance.   — *Marialis Cultis,* 1974

**Social Pressures on the Family**   To accept Christian life as a program becomes a difficult exercise today. The traditional way of life of our homes, orderly, simple and austere, good and happy, is no longer able to hold its own. Public morals, the protection of domestic and social virtues, are changing, and from certain standpoints, disappearing. Legality seems to be, but is not always, sufficient for the demands of morality. The family is challenged in its fundamental laws: unity, exclusiveness, perennity.   — Papal audience, March 19, 1975

**God's Support of Married Couples**   He is near you, to transfigure your love, to enrich its values, already so great and noble, with the far more wonderful ones of His grace; near you, to make firm, stable and indissoluble, the bond that unites you in mutual dedication to each other for your whole lives.

He is near you, to sustain you amid the contradictions, the trials, the crises, which are inevitable in human life, but certainly not — as some dire, theoretical and practical viewpoints would suggest — insuperable, fatal, destroying love which is as strong as death (Song of Songs 8:6), which lasts and survives in its stupendous possibility of recreating itself every day, intact and immaculate.

He is near you, to help you to overcome the real dangers of selfishness, hidden in the secret depths of the soul as a consequence of original sin, but which have also been overcome by the cross and resurrection of Christ.

—Papal audience, March 27, 1975

**Exaggerated Emphasis on the Unitive Dimension of Marriage** And now our discourse leads us to call to your attention certain opinions emanating from current trends of thought and also from new perspectives opened by the council. The proponents of the above-mentioned trends, while eulogizing beyond measure the blessings of conjugal love and the personal perfection of the spouses, have gone so far as to relegate the fundamental good of offspring to the second place, if they do not ignore it entirely.

They regard married love as an element of such great importance even in law that they subordinate to it the very validity of the nuptial bond, thus opening the way to practically unrestricted divorce, as though, if love fails (or rather the initial amorous passion), the validity itself of the irrevocable marriage covenant, originating in the free and full consent of love, should also cease to exist.        —Address to the Roman Rota, February 9, 1976

**Consent Constitutes a Marriage**    The Christian teaching on the family, as you are well aware, can in no way admit a concept of conjugal love that would lead to ignoring or depreciating the value and significance of this well-known principle: *a marriage is constituted by the consent of the parties.* This principle is of the utmost importance in all traditional canonical and theological teaching, and it has frequently been presented by the magisterium of the Church as one of the chief points upon which are based the natural law as it applies to marriage and the Gospel precept as well.

It must be absolutely denied, then, that with the cessation of any subjective element, such as is especially conjugal love, the marriage no longer exists as a juridical reality, originating in a consent that is once and for all juridically effective. This reality, on the juridical level, continues to exist independently of love and endures even if the sentiments of love should have completely disappeared.

In fact, the spouses, by giving their free consent, have entered and are part of an objective order or "institution" which transcends and is independent of them, both by its nature and the laws proper to it.

Matrimony did not originate in man's free will: it was instituted by God, who willed that it be endowed and provided with its own laws. Married people for the most part voluntarily and gladly recognize and esteem these laws, and in any case they should accept them as for their own good and that of their children and of society. From a spontaneous sentiment, love becomes a binding obligation (cf. Eph 5:25).

—Address to the Roman Rota, February 9, 1976

## Conclusion

The countercultural discipline, balance, and holistic nature of *lectio divina* is ideal for a virtue such as chastity, which requires an intensive, multidimensional effort and commitment in order to sustain itself in an unfriendly environment. To facilitate a healthy and efficacious response, we need the outlet of prayer, the subconscious and memory formation and practical applications of meditation, the peaceful reassurance of contemplation, and the practicality of action. *Lectio* is not a self-centered activity; like chastity, it is ordered to the good of all under the guidance of the Holy Spirit.

When we reflect on chastity, the inherent balance and moderating tendencies of *lectio divina* steer us away from the extremes of rationalization and scrupulosity and the pitfalls of pride and discouragement. Paul's teachings provide an extra measure of equilibrium because he is scrupulous about considering all sides of the issue and taking his audience into consideration.

Further, Paul's repeated emphasis of key concepts and pastoral sensitivities in combination with his precise vocabulary and articulate prose ensure that we are unlikely to encounter significant misunderstandings. It may take us a while to get the full meaning of his counsel, and his theological insight may be beyond us for the moment, but we are unlikely to misinterpret him significantly. He usually follows up his crisp articulation with qualifiers or exemplification so that his point is understood and contextualized.

As a diplomat, Paul was keenly aware of the importance of precision and nuance in communications. As pope this led him to be very deliberate in his communications and decision-making. His gaunt, somber appearance along with his sensitivity and grasp of complexities made him appear conflicted, which on divisive issues he was.

Paul was ridiculed for being indecisive and then criticized for his decisions, yet the same critics failed to notice both pastoral and doctrinal nuances and qualifying statements in his teachings that made them more palatable for people in challenging circumstances.

Paul and *lectio,* and their fundamental sources, God's word and life experience, can help us navigate the journey of chastity. Let us not get discouraged when we stumble en route, knowing that our growth and healing occurs within the providence of a loving and merciful God who withholds nothing good from us, including the gift of sexuality (cf. Rom 8:31–32).

# Chapter 10

# Human Development

*Once more we reiterate our good wish: Advance always!...*

*It does not suffice, however, to feed the hungry; it is necessary also to assure to each man a life conformed to his dignity....*

*We intend to intensify the development of our charitable institutions to combat world hunger and fulfill world needs. It is thus, and in no other way, that peace can be built up....*

*The hour has struck for our "conversion," for personal transformation, for interior renewal. We must get used to thinking of man in a new way; also of men's life in common; with a new manner too of conceiving the paths of history and the destiny of the world, according to the words of St. Paul: "You must be clothed in the new self, which is created in God's image, justified and sanctified through the truth" (Eph 4.23).*

*The hour has struck for a halt, a moment of recollection, of reflection, almost of prayer. A moment to think anew of our common origin, our history, our common destiny.*

*Today as never before, in our era so marked by human progress, there is need for an appeal to the moral conscience of man. For the danger comes, not from progress, nor from science — indeed, if properly utilized, these could rather resolve many of the grave problems which assail mankind. No, the real danger comes from man himself, wielding ever more powerful arms which could be employed equally well for destruction or for the loftiest conquests.*

—Pope Paul VI, Address to the
U.N. General Assembly, October 4, 1965

On March 26, 1967, Pope Paul VI issued an encyclical entitled *Populorum Progressio* ("On the Development of Peoples"), which along with a 1971 apostolic letter entitled *Octogesima Adveniens* ("A Call to Action") updated and in some ways revolutionized Catholic social teaching.

These prophetic documents explored individual, social, and cultural development, especially third world issues, in light of Catholic social teaching. Many of the quotations in this section are from *Populorum Progressio,* including what John Paul II called its "historic label": "Development is the new name for peace."

We could also have entitled this chapter "human dignity." Respect for human dignity is likewise the new name for peace. An intrinsic link between human development and dignity permeates the teachings of Paul VI and John Paul II.

In his 1991 encyclical *Sollicitudo Rei Socialis* ("On Social Concern"), John Paul II discussed *Populorum Progressio* at length and termed it distinguished, original, and of enduring relevance. Benedict XVI likewise referenced it in his 2006 message for Lent and in his first encyclical *Deus Est Caritas* ("God Is Love.")

Human science authorities have also sung its praises. Hervé Carrier, S.J., former secretary of the Pontifical Council for Culture, described this "famous" encyclical as "on the culture of human progress" and observed that it was viewed by some as a major event in civilization. On its publication, the economist François Perroux commented: "It is one of the greatest texts in human history. It radiates a kind of rational, moral, and religious testimony."

Along with *Ecclesiam Suam* ("Paths of the Church"), *Humanae Vitae* ("On Human Life"), and *Evangelii Nuntiandi* ("On Evangelization in the Modern World"), *Populorum Progressio* is regarded as among Paul VI's most prophetic, influential, and enduring documents. It is the favorite of many admirers of Paul VI and is the cornerstone of post–Vatican II Catholic social teaching.

## The Development of Paul's Teaching

*Octogesima Adveniens* updated its predecessor in response to a rapidly changing world. The liberation theology movement in Latin America was gaining influence, and both Africa and Asia were beset with civil wars and widespread poverty. In its application of the principle of subsidiarity to social justice issues, *Octogesima Adveniens* followed Paul's decentralizing tendencies and offered guidelines for adapting *Populorum Progressio*'s teachings to local situations.

While such global issues exceed the direct influence of most of us, these documents also have compelling personal applications, beginning with the link Paul identified between individual and communal development.

This is very relevant in today's individualistic, self-centered culture where emphasis is on self-actualization and personal fulfillment in dependent of the common good. Rare is the self-help book that integrates social consciousness, orthodox spirituality, and morality with credible input from the human sciences. Paul's insights into spirituality, culture, and potential fulfillment are a credible alternative to pop psychology and New Age spirituality, and thus have evangelical as well as developmental and therapeutic applications

Paul insisted that human development was a religious as well as human vocation. It is an obligation rather than an option. Such is part of God's plan as echoed throughout the Bible and Christian tradition: e.g., "You must be perfect as my heavenly father is perfect" (cf. Mt 5:48) and St. Irenaeus's famous observation that "man fully alive is the glory of God."

Rejecting the rationalization and irresponsibility that has plagued modern society and popular psychology, Paul VI points out that while development is influenced considerably by external factors, it remains primarily the responsibility of the individual. He is not letting us off the hook.

## Paul VI as Motivational Guru

Implications for human development and fulfillment pervade the entire corpus of Paul's teachings, so look for them throughout this book. Along with John Paul II, Paul VI is among Catholicism's finest teachers on the subject.

When we read Paul's words there are times we have to remind ourselves that the message is from a pope and not a motivational speaker. (Of course, his integrity, humility, and shyness would have ruled out any sort of pope-fomercial.) Most important, he lived the message and inspired others as well.

Paul VI was not a narrow, compartmentalized thinker. As manifested in his frequently noted deliberateness when making a decision, Paul struggled to balance macro (the whole or "big picture") and micro (individual) issues in the interests of the common good. Because he did not oversimplify, he recognized subtleties and complexities and the necessity of nuanced responses. His balanced, pastoral approach is necessary, if not necessarily appreciated, in today's complex world.

Along with his reserved public persona and subsequent inability to project his personal charm and charisma to a large audience, these characteristics help explain his relative unpopularity with the masses. His namesake, St. Paul, was also criticized for his unimpressive stature and oratory (cf. 2 Cor 10:10). Mass society prefers simple, convenient answers, but these rarely suffice for the challenges of life.

In the spirit of 1 Tm 4:1–5, which warned against false teachers who denied the goodness of creation, Pope Paul affirms everything that is authentically human. Balancing such enthusiasm is his prudence and discretion. He cautions us to avoid the extremes of angelism (denial of bodily realities), utopianism, hedonism, and cynicism.

Balance, the maintenance of opposites in a healthy tension, is a key to understanding Paul, human development, and ourselves. Each of us is a study in contrasts and polarities that require moderation and integration.

Like St. Augustine, whose writings were pivotal in the formation of his spirituality, Paul was deeply aware of human weakness and resistance to God's will. As mentioned, he often preceded his moral exhortations with the expression "whether we like it or not." Paul teaches as one of us and not from a palatial tower.

## Paul's Developmental Path

Paul's potential fulfillment journey spanned his whole life. His social, cultural, and developmental aptitudes were established early. His father was a non-practicing attorney as well as a newspaper editor and social activist, and his mother, to whom he was very close, led an active life. His sickly childhood and strict upbringing provided him with a sense of the importance of efficiency and effectiveness. He became a widely respected scholar and diplomat although he never received a university degree. As Pius XII's pro-secretary of state, he advocated time cards in the curia, more responsible use of long distance telephone calls, and punctuality.

Paul's industriousness did not compromise his graciousness. He never became impersonal or overbearing in his diligence. Although he worked long hours, overcommitted himself, and invariably fell behind schedule, he never rushed his appointments, always giving them his undivided attention. Paul's insights into human development are so abundant, instructive, and inspiring that together with joy and chastity, subjects on which he was particularly prophetic and pastoral, they constitute the longest chapters in this book.

## An Exhortation for the Ages

My favorite piece of writing from Paul VI is the excerpt from his testament that concludes this section. This profound statement circulated informally among clergy and religious. A priest who lived in Rome when Paul became pope shared it with me. He was present when Paul gave Mary the title "Mother of the Church" in November 1964 as a way of appeasing conservatives who were disappointed that discussion of her was included as a concluding chapter in the Dogmatic Constitution on the Church, *Lumen Gentium* ("Light to the Nations") rather than in a separate document.

In November 2001, when I had the opportunity to conduct research at the Paolo VI Istituto in Brescia, Italy, Paul's birthplace, I was able to purchase several copies of a limited edition book that reproduced Paul's will both in his original handwriting and in typeset Italian.

I frequently refer to this excerpt for my own inspiration and others'. I hope it proves transformational for you as well.

# HUMAN DEVELOPMENT

**The Preeminence of Morality in Human Action**   The moral consideration in human action should be neither omitted nor discredited; it is the highest and most noble consideration in human action, the most personal and indispensable.

We should remember that the moral sense, the disposition to consider our own actions and those of others in the light of integrity, is not only the best ornament for each individual, but is also a nation's most precious and civilizing heritage.

—Lent, 1961

**Religion Encompasses Work and Life**   Work, however profane or material, is guided by another spiritual faculty of man, the will. This in its turn gives human activity a moral qualification; this qualification, whether we like it or not, derives its own genuine vitality from duty; and duty postulates the relationship of man with his ultimate aim, God....

All this shows us how the opposition which has grown up between religion and labor derives chiefly from a restricted concept often held of religion. One is apt to consider religion as just one of man's many activities, limited to a specific field, to its outer forms, to certain definite moments; such a concept would be enough for an activity that was only human.

But religion takes the whole sweep of life, all the horizons of reality, into its vision. It not only traces connections between component parts, it describes the whole arch of the general order.... Everything is included in the universal conception it puts forward.                                      —March 1960

**Catholic Optimism**   In Rome there is a logic of expectation, developing and reaching out toward new aims; there is a premise which could be a promise: here nothing is ended, all is beginning; here the petitions of human needs find their supreme court of appeal. The trust in, the art of, human perfectibility have their stronghold, their workshop in Rome. Pessimism has no place on her soil. Here redemption is always possible; here peace can always be achieved, human progress always pursued.

A genuine humanism seems in constant development here; in the words of the Bible, "Let us make man in the likeness of God" (Gen 1:26) — that is, according to man's highest prototype. The effort is never satisfied by the results, and that in itself suggests a course of action; for here Christ is in the process of becoming — "until Christ is formed in us" (Gal 4:19).

—Easter, 1962

**Love of Work**    It is necessary to love work. The desire to work in order to earn one's daily bread is legitimate and I would say sacred.                                 —Papal audience, October 19, 1963

**The Discipline of the Cross**    Christianity is a training ground for the moral powers, it is a school of self-discipline, it is an enterprise involving courage and heroism precisely because it does not fear to teach a man temperance, self-control, generosity, self-denial and sacrifice; and because it knows and teaches that the true and perfect man, the pure and strong man, the man capable of acting and of loving is a student of the discipline of Christ: the discipline of the Cross.

—Papal audience, February 12, 1964

**The Gospel's Realistic Humanism**    The Gospel, which recognizes, denounces, pities and cures human misfortunes with penetrating and sometimes with heart — rending sincerity, does not yield to any illusions about the natural goodness of man (as if he were sufficient unto himself and as if he needed nothing else than to be left free to express himself according to his whims), nor to any despairing resignation to the incurable corruption of human nature.                  —*Ecclesiam Suam*, 1964

**The Dignity of Work**    To be a worker is a sign of reliability. It is a respectable qualification. Indeed it does you credit and honor.

Being workmen means that you take life seriously, that you know what duty means, that you know the value of time, of money, of toil, and that you have an immediate idea of the world in which we live, a world which makes work a law of life, an obligation for all, a principle of personal social development, a duty and an honor.                  —Papal audience, January 5, 1965

**Obedience Perfects Liberty**    Obedience does not suffocate one's liberty, but rather perfects it; it stimulates activity and exults the human person. Disobedience, on the other hand, disperses energies and makes man the slave of his passions.

— Papal audience, November 20, 1965

**Humankind's Twofold Potential**    The attention of our council has been absorbed by the discovery of human needs (and these needs grow in proportion to the greatness which the son of the earth claims for himself). But we call upon those who term themselves modern humanists, and who have renounced the transcendent value of the highest realities, to give the council credit at least for one quality and to recognize our own new type of humanism: we, too, in fact, we more than any others, honor mankind.

And what aspect of humanity has this august senate studied? What goal under divine inspiration did it set for itself? It also dwelt upon humanity's ever twofold facet, namely, man's wretchedness and his greatness, his profound weakness — which is undeniable and cannot be cured by himself — and the good that survives in him which is ever marked by a hidden beauty and an invincible serenity.

— Closing session, Vatican Council II, December 7, 1965

**Council Optimism**    But one must realize that this council, which exposed itself to human judgment, insisted very much more upon this pleasant side of man, rather than on his unpleasant one. Its attitude was very much and deliberately optimistic.

— Closing session, Vatican Council II, December 7, 1965

**The Church Is on Humanity's Side**    Hence no one should ever say that a religion like the Catholic religion is without use, seeing that when it has its greatest self-awareness and effectiveness, as it has in council, it declares itself entirely on the side of man and in his service. In this way the Catholic religion and human life reaffirm their alliance with one another, the fact that they converge on one single human reality: the Catholic religion is for mankind. In a certain sense it is the life of mankind.

It is so by the extremely precise and sublime interpretation that our religion gives of humanity (surely man by himself is a mystery to himself) and gives this interpretation in virtue of its knowledge of God: a knowledge of God is a prerequisite for a knowledge of man as he really is, in all his fullness; for proof of this let it suffice for now to recall the ardent expression of St. Catherine of Siena, "In your nature, Eternal God, I shall know my own." —Closing session, Vatican Council II, December 7, 1965

**Christian Humanism** The Catholic religion is man's life because it determines life's nature and destiny; it gives life its real meaning, it establishes the supreme law of life and infuses it with that mysterious activity which we may say divinizes it.

Consequently, if we remember, venerable brothers and all of you, our children, gathered here, how in everyone we can and must recognize the countenance of Christ (cf. Mt 25:40), the Son of Man, especially when tears and sorrows make it plain to see, and if we can and must recognize in Christ's countenance the countenance of our heavenly Father "He who sees me," Our Lord said, "sees also the Father" (Jn 14:9), our humanism becomes Christianity, our Christianity becomes centered on God; in such sort that we may say, to put it differently: a knowledge of man is a prerequisite for a knowledge of God.
—Closing session, Vatican Council II, December 7, 1965

**The Duty of Thinking** But do not forget that if thinking is something great, it is first a duty. Woe to him who voluntarily closes his eyes to the light. Thinking is also a responsibility, so woe to those who darken the spirit by the thousand tricks which degrade it, make it proud, deceive and deform it. What other basic principle is there for men of science except to think rightly? —Closing speech, Vatican Council II, December 8, 1965

**Human Fulfillment Is a Christian Duty** By the unaided effort of his own intelligence and his will, each man can grow in humanity, can enhance his personal worth, can become more a person. However, this self-fulfillment is not something optional.

Just as the whole of creation is ordained to its Creator, so spiritual beings should of their own accord orientate their lives to God, the first truth and the supreme good. Thus it is that human fulfillment constitutes, as it were, a summary of our duties.

—*Populorum Progressio,* 1967

**The World Needs Beauty**    This world in which we live needs beauty in order not to sink into despair. It is beauty, like truth, which brings joy to the heart of man and is that precious fruit which resists the wear and tear of time, which unites generations and makes them share things in admiration.

—Closing speech, Vatican Council II, December 8, 1965

**Union with Christ Perfects Humanity**    But there is much more: this harmonious enrichment of nature by personal and responsible effort is ordered to a further perfection. By reason of his union with Christ, the source of life, man attains to new fulfillment of himself, to a transcendent humanism which gives him his greatest possible perfection: this is the highest goal of personal development.                    —*Populorum Progressio,* 1967

**Targeting a Complete Humanism**    What must be aimed at is complete humanism. And what is that if not the fully rounded development of the whole man and of all men?

A humanism closed in on itself, and not open to the values of the spirit and to God Who is their source, could achieve apparent success. True, man can organize the world apart from God, but "without God man can organize it in the end only to man's detriment. An isolated humanism is an inhuman humanism."

—*Populorum Progressio,* 1967

**True Humanism Is Transcendent**    There is no true humanism but that which is open to the Absolute and is conscious of a vocation which gives human life its true meaning. Far from being the ultimate measure of all things, man can only realize himself by reaching beyond himself. As Pascal has said so well: "Man infinitely surpasses man."                    —*Populorum Progressio,* 1967

**A Sense of Meaning, Mission, and Destiny**   The Church is Christ's theatre. Every believer may here have a sense of the meaning and value of his own existence, and may feel himself to give his own life a mission of its own, a destiny which is human and superhuman at the same time.

—Papal audience, March 14, 1968

**Work Bears the Imprint of the Worker**   Christian thought, which is that of the Church, considers work as the expression of the human faculties, both physical and spiritual, which impress on manual labor the mark of human personality, and consequently its progress, its perfection, and in the end its economic and social utility.

Work is the normal exercise of the human qualities, physical, moral and spiritual, so that it clothes the dignity, the talent, the perfecting and productive genius of man.

—Papal audience, May 1, 1968

**The Sacredness of Work**   It [work] obeys the primordial design of God the Creator, who wished man to be the explorer, conqueror, ruler of the earth, of its treasures, energies and secrets. Therefore, work is not of itself punishment, decadence, or the yoke of slavery, as it was considered by ancient peoples, even the best of them. It is the expression of the natural need of man to use his powers, to measure them against difficulties, to make nature serve him....

Labor therefore is noble, and like every honest human activity, it is sacred.   —Papal audience, May 1, 1968

**Workers Deserve Their Wages — and Leisure**   Progressively better working conditions must be brought about, to change the sad and humiliated face of labor, to give it a truly new aspect — humane, strong, free, serene, lighted by the conquest not only of economic benefits sufficient for a healthy and worthwhile life, but of the higher benefits of culture, leisure, the legitimate joy of living and Christian hope.   —Papal audience, May 1, 1968

**Imitating Christ, the Model of Human Perfection**   The Christian, if he really is one, is the true man, he is the man who realizes himself fully and freely, and he does this by modeling himself on an example of infinite perfection and of unsurpassed humanity, Christ our Lord, who can be imitated in those necessary ways required by faith and grace, as well as in many other ways suggested by a man's own mental make-up as a Christian and by his own conscious choice.      —Papal audience, July 17, 1968

**The Council and Christian Humanism**      The council throughout puts before the Christian a wise humanism which, without forgetting the great laws of evangelical perfection, such as the renunciations which make us more holy and more spiritual or the sacrifices which imprint on our life the redemptive sign of the Cross, raise the Christian to the stature of the complete man, to the fullness of the gifts received, together with life itself, from God, to the ordered balance of his faculties, to the unwearied and harmonious employment of his powers, to the community sense in his actual relationships, to the dignity of his own conscience, not certainly as a criterion of a free and responsible moral conduct.

It is good that actually in our own day, so disturbed as it is by ideological and social confusion, the Church of God speaks to each and all of perfection, the human, moral perfection of everyday life.                              —Papal audience, July 17, 1968

**Penance and Perfection**      The need to direct one's life definitely Godward and in accordance with His will, the necessity of self-control and purification in one's life, the reasonableness of a basic choice which will give shape and moral worth to one's conduct, the pressing inner need to make good one's failings (cf. *L'Innominato* of Manzoni), the secret attraction to come close to the Cross of Christ and to integrate His sufferings into one's own flesh (cf. Col 1:24), these today, and always where the Gospel is accepted and lived up to, give to penance a role for which there can be no substitute in the ideal make-up of the true man, of man in search of perfection.              —Papal audience, July 24, 1968

**Penance Restores Goodness**      Things that call for strength, great things, things that are beautiful, perfect, these are difficult and require renunciation, effort, care, patience, sacrifice. Christian penance is for the new man, the perfect man. It is functional; it is not an end in itself. It does not lessen a man; it is an art whereby he is restored to his primeval likeness, that which reflects the image of God which God had in mind when He created man (Gen 1:26–27).

It is an art whereby, after the afflictions of penance, there is imprinted on the countenance of man the paschal splendor of the risen Christ. That is our humanism.

It seems like a paradox. But it wins out over the grotesque disfigurement of human beauty aimed at in the "dolce vita." It cures the wounds and dries the tears with which suffering has marred the face of man; it restores to our life the security it longs for and more and more lacks, the security of perfection in immortality. "He who hath ears to hear, let him hear" (cf. Mk 4:23; Mt 19:12).                        —Papal audience, July 24, 1968

**Christian versus Secular Concepts of Perfection**    But the search for the ideal man differs greatly in the two concepts, the Christian and the profane. (This is a practical classification in this simple discourse.) We can get the difference between the two concepts both as regards human perfection and the ways of obtaining it, particularly from the pedagogical field where teachers work for the formation of the true, complete and perfect man.

Let us note in passing how the two concepts run through the itinerary of life in contrary directions. The Christian ideal begins with the known premise of the dignity of man and his perfectibility, but based at the same time on a two-fold negative observation: the one derives from his inheritance of original sin which has weakened the very nature of man, giving rise to a lack of balance, deficiencies and weakness of his faculties.

The other denies the ability of human power alone to reach the true perfection which is necessary to man's salvation, namely, his sharing in the life of God through grace. And from these premises the concept of Christian perfection unfolds itself as a victory achieved through grace and a patient practice of the natural and supernatural virtues. Perfection becomes possible, progressive and certain of final fulfillment.

— Papal audience, August 7, 1968

**Interior Renewal Is the Seed of Christian Perfection** "Be transformed by the renewal of your mind" (Rom 12:2). And this is the most necessary reform and the most difficult.

Change your thoughts, your tastes, according to the Will of God; correct those faults that we often boast of as our principles and qualities; search for a continual interior uprightness of feelings and resolutions. Let yourselves be really guided by the love of God and, consequently, by the love of your neighbor.

Listen truly to the word of the Lord, and accustom yourself to hear the voice of the Holy Spirit with humility and interior silence, nourish that "sense of the Church" that makes it easy for you to understand how much of the divine and how much of the human is in it.

Make yourselves available with simplicity and a spirit of sacrifice that facilitates charity and the generous following of Christ. This is the reform which, before every other, is demanded of us.

— Papal audience, August 7, 1968

**Understanding Conscience and Liberty** With reference to the exaltation of the human person on the part of the Church's doctrines and charisms, two points ought to be particularly dear to contemporary humanism: conscience and liberty.... A right understanding of them is difficult.

The superficial vocabulary current in our times prevents many from having an exact concept of either conscience or of liberty, and much less so, of their right use. Both terms deserve a careful study....

But the fact remains that the Church vindicates man's conscience and liberty in the highest and most exact sense. In so doing, the Church confers on man a stature she describes as "creature," but a creature made in the image of God, the Creator. This creature, elevated into the ineffable love of Christian regeneration, is raised to the level of son and of participant of the divine nature (cf. 2 Pt 1:4).    — Papal audience, September 4, 1968

**Be the Best You Can Be** The Church needs saints. The world needs saints. There is need of saints whose imitation of Christ and the tradition of the Church teach us that their lives were difficult and sweet; saints who in the tumult of modern experience, of current ideologies, of fashionable controversies, know how to be at once personally and socially free from the collective mimicry, and spontaneously and firmly consecrated to the service of God and their brethren. Make of your life, dearest sons, a total experience in sanctity. Settle not for halfway measures nor content yourselves with mediocre compromise, nor give yourselves up to the influences of the formidable which surrounds us. —Papal audience, October 27, 1968

**Christian Perfection Is Realized Humanity** But let no one take fright. For the perfection to which we are called by our Christian election does not complicate and aggravate life, even if it requires us to observe many practical norms, calculated rather to help our faithfulness than to make it more difficult.

Christian perfection demands from us above all an inquiry into the fundamental principles of our human being. Our duty seeks to equate itself with our being. We should be what we are. This is the principle of natural law, about which there is so much discussion today, but which mere reason vindicates in its fundamental demands. These demands are derived from life itself, and they are interpreted by common sense, ordinary reason. It is the law we bear in ourselves, as men: "a law not written, but innate" (Cicero); the law that St. Paul recognizes also in peoples to whom the Mosaic law was not announced (cf. Rom 2:14), and which the Gospel has absorbed, confirmed and perfected. —Papal audience, March 4, 1970

**Think for Yourself!** But the modernity of a doctrine is not enough in itself to endow it with credibility. Those who let themselves be carried along by fashions in thinking and mass opinions are often not aware that their attitude is a servile one. They enthuse about the words and ideas of others, and of convenient opinions. They make no mental effort of their own; they rejoice to feel that they have been freed from the mentality of their surroundings (which is often not without wisdom and experience); they let themselves be carried away by triumphant ideas of others. They think they are free!

— Papal audience, August 5, 1970

**Living the Natural Virtues**    Should not a Christian distinguish himself in living the fundamental natural virtues, for example, sincerity and justice? Or course he should! More, we should hope that Christian upbringing will always be more and more marked by the awareness and observances of these natural virtues, such as respect for the truth in word and deed, and devotion to justice especially in social relations.

— Papal audience, March 18, 1970

**Mining the Truth**    The truth remains, but it is demanding. We must know it, we must study it, we must purify its human expressions. What a renewal this implies! The truth remains, but it is a fruitful truth. No one can ever say that he has fully comprehended and defined it in the formulas whose meaning however remains untouchable. It can present aspects still worthy of research. . . .

The truth remains, but it needs to be made known, translated and formulated, in a way suited to the pupils' capacity for understanding. . . .

Religion is therefore open to being perfected, increased, deepened. It is a science which is always engaged in a sublime effort, striving toward better understanding or to a better mode of expression.                   — Papal audience, August 12, 1970

**Situation Ethics, Conscience, and Objective Norms**    Another simplification consists in maintaining that conduct is governed by the situation in which we find ourselves. You have all heard this. Certainly, the circumstances, the situation, are an element which conditions the human act. But this act may not prescind from higher and objective moral norms, though the situation itself can mean justifying opportunism, inconsistency, cowardice. So forget about character, heroism and true moral law? Man's existence may not overlook his essence. . . .

Not to mention that conscience, to which situation morality appeals, conscience, alone and unenlightened by transcendent principles, unguided by an authoritative magisterium, cannot be the fallible arbiter of the morality of an action. The conscience is an eye which needs light. —Papal audience, October 7, 1970

**Authentic Progress** Certainly in the face of difficulties to be overcome there is a great temptation to use one's authority to diminish the number of guests rather than to multiply the bread that is to be shared . . . the Church, on her part, in every domain of human action encourages scientific and technical progress, but always claiming respect for the inviolable right of the human person whose primary guarantors are the public authorities.

Being firmly opposed to a birth control which according to the just expression of our venerable predecessor Pope John XXIII would be in accordance with "methods and means which are unworthy of man," the Church calls all those responsible to work with fearlessness and generosity for the development of the whole man and every man; this, among other effects will undoubtedly favor a rational control of birth by couples who are capable of freely assuming their destiny.
—Conference of the Food and Agriculture Organization, November 16, 1970

**Wisdom Liberates** We want to be liberated from those illusions, frustrations, injustices and repressions to which the modern world has subjected us in violation of its promises — this is what the young are saying, the disinherited, the automatons of modern technology: we want to be free persons, real men, people rescued from hunger and from the spiral of incurable inferiority.

Yes, answers the Man of men: come to me all you who are in tribulation and I will console you. I am with you, with the power of the Spirit, not with the violence of force and passion. Wisdom alone liberates the world. —Christmas Message, 1970

**Action and Energy** In the contemporary world we see everyone running; that is, we see that human activity has speeded up its rhythm to an impressive extent. Action is preeminent among all human values. What is important today is to get more and more things done. To move about, to change, to produce, to enjoy, is the order of the day.

Intensity of operation is the yardstick to judge the merit of a person, a society, or an instrument, any organized system. Energy has the first place among desirable things. So power, speed, novelty, revolution head the list of current evaluations. The whirl of events feeds common attention; public opinion longs for the continuous, traumatic excitement of a continuous succession of happenings.                —Papal audience, March 10, 1971

**Dedication to a Cause**   Life must be dedicated to a great cause. We cannot remain inert and insensitive.

—Papal audience, March 12, 1971

**There Is No True Humanism without God**   For us believers, there can be no doubt: a humanism closed within itself, excluding God, will turn out sooner or later to be inhuman.

Why? Because God remains the source and the term of the supreme values without which man cannot live. Because the realities of sin and of death and the questions they raise, for each man as well as for history, do not receive a radical and definitive solution outside faith.        —Papal audience, March 18, 1971

**Remaking the City and Culture**   It is in fact the weakest who are the victims of dehumanizing living conditions, degrading for conscience and harmful for the family institution. The promiscuity of working people's housing makes a minimum of intimacy impossible; young couples waiting in vain for a decent dwelling at a price they can afford are demoralized and their union can thereby even be endangered; youth escape from a home which is too confined and seek in the streets compensations and companionships which cannot be supervised. It is the grave duty of those responsible to strive to control this process and to give it direction.

There is an urgent need to remake at the level of the street, of the neighborhood or of the great agglomerative dwellings the social fabric whereby man may be able to develop the needs of his personality. Centers of special interest and of culture must be created or developed at the community and parish levels with different forms of associations, recreational centers, and spiritual and community gatherings where the individual can escape from isolation and form anew fraternal relationships.

— *Octogesima Adveniens*, 1971

**The Limitations of Scientific Analysis**  In this world dominated by scientific and technological change, which threatens to drag it toward a new posivitism, another more fundamental doubt is raised. Having subdued nature by using his reason, man now finds that he himself is as it were imprisoned within his own rationality; he in turn becomes the object of science.

The "human sciences" are today enjoying a significant flowering. On the one hand they are subjecting to critical and radical examination the hitherto accepted knowledge about man, on the grounds that this knowledge seems either too empirical or too theoretical. On the other hand, methodological necessity and ideological presuppositions too often lead the human sciences to isolate, in the various situations, certain aspects of man, and yet to give these an explanation which claims to be complete or at least an interpretation which is meant to be all-embracing from a purely quantitative or phenomenological point of view.

This scientific reduction betrays a dangerous presupposition. To give a privileged position in this way to such an aspect of analysis is to mutilate man and, under the pretext of a scientific procedure, to make it impossible to understand man in his totality.           — *Octogesima Adveniens*, 1971

**The Call to Action**  It is to all Christians that we address a fresh and insistent call to action. In our encyclical on the Development of Peoples we urged that all should set themselves to the task: "Laymen should take up as their own proper task the renewal of the temporal order.

"If the role of the hierarchy is to teach and to interpret authentically the norms of morality to be followed in this matter, it belongs to the laity, without waiting passively for orders and directives, to take the initiatives freely and to infuse a Christian spirit into the mentality, customs, laws and structures of the community in which they live."

Let each one examine himself, to see what he has done up to now, and what he ought to do. It is not enough to recall principles, state intentions, point to crying injustice and utter prophetic denunciations; these words will lack real weight unless they are accompanied for each individual by a livelier awareness of personal responsibility and by effective action.

It is too easy to throw back on others responsibility for injustice, if at the same time one does not realize how each one shares in it personally, and how personal conversion is needed first. This basic humility will rid action of all inflexibility and sectarianism, it will also avoid discouragement in the face of a task which seems limitless in size.

Thus, amid the diversity of situations, functions and organizations, each one must determine, in his conscience, the actions which he is called to share in. Surrounded by various currents into which, besides legitimate aspirations, there insinuate themselves more ambiguous tendencies, the Christian must make a wise and vigilant choice and avoid involving himself in collaboration without conditions and contrary to the principles of a true humanism, even in the name of a genuinely felt solidarity.

*— Octogesima Adveniens,* 1971

**Christian Activism**    Man's worth lies, we could say in the last resort, not so much in what he is, but in what he does....

The school of the Gospel, updated in awareness and in methods, tends to make man an activist. The Gospel can be read in the key of "action." Action is the conscious and desired development of being, its perfection, its happiness.

*—* Papal audience, July 7, 1971

**The Gospel and Human Development**    The whole Gospel is a treatise on the development of man (how often the parable of the seed recurs!); and the liberating announcement of the kingdom is completely interwoven with duties to be performed, choosing the narrow and hard way (cf. Mt 7:14), without falling back because of fatigue or obstacles (cf. Lk 9:62), to the extent of giving one's own life, if necessary (Jn 12:25)!

The Gospel is not a code that is easily carried out; it calls for effort and faithfulness. —Papal audience, July 7, 1971

**The Council's Balanced Humanism** Does the Christian conception, we ask ourselves, fall into a similar one-sided view of things, giving exclusive preference to religious values?

Does the council, perhaps, restrict its anthropological doctrine merely to consideration of man's relationship with God? No, it does not.

On the contrary, in its teachings, the council (and this is one of its original characteristics) assigns, and almost demands, for all natural values, an esteem of their own, a function of their own. From this point of view, the Church has been magnanimous and courageous: she has opened her eyes and therefore given her respectful recognition to all the aspects of man, that many-sided being.... She has proclaimed and defended every legitimate right of man.

Hence Christian humanism. The whole council speaks of it.

Let us quote, in conclusion, one sentence: "There is a growing awareness of the exalted dignity proper to the human person, since he stands above all things, and his rights and duties are universal and inviolable...the ferment of the Gospel, too, has aroused and continues to arouse in man's heart the irresistible requirements of his dignity." —Papal audience, July 28, 1971

**Purpose in Life** What is life? What qualifies it essentially?

From this elementary, but fundamental questions comes a first answer, which is worth remembering; life is made for action; it is not static, it is dynamic; it changes, develops, moves, seeks, desires, works, aims at some goal.

It is not enough to exist; it is necessary to use existence to reach something new, something more, something perfect, good and happy.

If experience has awakened in us this conception of life in search of a purpose, we have arrived at the threshold of the moral problem, the human problem per excellence. If action, in fact, which gives increase and meaning to life, uses what is most human in us, thought, will, and therefore freedom, then to speak of a moral and to speak of a human act is the same thing.

— Papal audience, July 5, 1972

**Balancing Progress**   But let us conclude at once with two observations, or rather two exhortations.

The first one: we must realize without fear and without inner mistrust of our times, that Providence has caused us to be born in a historic hour such as ours; characterized, we were saying, by change and progress. Let us try to understand this condition of developing humanity, and let us bless with a wise and open heart the good things that human effort offers human life.

The second one: let us keep our balance at the changes that are taking place around us; or rather, let us try to discover in them a need, far more logical, of higher principles to support the movements in which we are engaged, in order that the latter may be neither overpowering, nor anarchical, nor amorphous, but rather invincible and impelled to traverse, in time, the ways of God, which must lead us beyond time.

— Papal audience, July 5, 1972

**Conduct Is Preeminent**   We need to find again the principles on which our conduct must be based.

Let us recall in the meantime that our conduct is the most important thing in our life. If being, in other words, living, is the supreme value subjectively for us, then action, the use of our life, is our supreme duty.

Everything depends on what we all do together. Fundamental, particularly for us Christians, who have a specific conception of life: our ultimate and definitive fate will depend on what we have done.

Let us remember the parable of the talents. We can consider talents, that is, the gifts of life, what we are, as our fortune, but at the same time as our responsibility; our salvation will depend on the use we make of them. Life is like a ship; what is important for a ship is the rudder, where it is going, the direction it takes, the harbor for which it is bound. This rudder is moral judgment, or rather the moral imperative.     —Papal audience, July 14, 1972

**Educating the Will**   We wish to recall the three moments of the good will as they appear to us in turning over once again the golden pages of St. Thomas Aquinas concerning the nature of the voluntary act.

The first moment concerns the intention. In order to act well we must before all else have the right intention, which awakens the will and directs it to the thing desired as good, by reason of the good which it represents. This rectitude reaches out beyond the thing itself to the Supreme Good, to the ultimate end, which subordinates to itself in hierarchical order every virtuous good.

Then comes the moment of choice, of decision, of love, when the soul moves itself with liberty and power, with a capacity to make great sacrifices for the sake of great conquests.

Finally there is the third moment, that of execution, of command, of practical activity, with all the virtues it requires, the so-called cardinal virtues, because under them are arranged and organized human actions directed to the good.

Having said all this we should realize that we have omitted in this very brief exposition an operative factor of transcendent and indispensable importance: the grace of God! Divine grace infuses into us the very capacity "to will and to do" precisely in relation to the good will (cf. Phil 2:13). It is a marvel and a mystery of the Christian life. . . .

Now that we must bring this discourse to an end, we cannot refrain from exhorting everyone, who has the sense of his own Christian calling, to reflect on the importance of education of the will in order to avoid the situation, on the last day, where our gift of life, and still more of the Christian life might be laid to our charge as an unfulfilled responsibility, if for no other reason than a fatal sin of omission (cf. Mt 25:31ff.). That is the dreadful eschatological condemnation of Christ the judge: "When you have not done (the good that you should have done to your neighbor in need), you have not done it to me!" (cf. also 2 Pt 2:21).     —Papal audience, August 23, 1972

**Christianity Rejects Mediocrity**    The program of Christian life does not tolerate mediocrity. Terrible, in this connection, are the words of Revelation, which says: "I know your works; you are neither cold nor hot. . . . So because you are lukewarm, I will spew you out of my mouth" (Rev 3:15–16).

The first Christians, admitted to the ecclesial communion of faith and grace, were called holy in name, and they knew that they had to behave as such. This mentality, which makes it obligatory to conform one's way of life to the demands of the new style of life, Christian style, is still cultivated in new missionary communities today.    —Papal audience, November 4, 1972

**Periodic Self-Analysis**    We can be content, now, to express in practical terms this austere word "conversion," calling it "interior reform." We are called to this reform: which at once makes us understand many things.

The first concerns the interior analysis of our spirit; yes, a kind of religious and moral psychoanalysis. We must withdraw within ourselves to examine what is the real principal direction of our life, that is, what is the usual and prevalent motive of our way of thinking and acting, what is our reason for living, what is the moral style of our personality: can we call ourselves honest men, consistent and faithful Christians? Are we steering toward the right goal? Or does our course need to be rectified?

—Papal audience, March 21, 1973

**Drawing Up a Spiritual Balance Sheet**    In this connection, too, secular life offers a model for spiritual life: do we not draw up annual balance sheets of our economic administrations? How is our business getting on? And the business of religious and moral life? Is not Lenten discipline, especially if strengthened by the so-called "spiritual exercises," entirely directed at controlling the fundamental uprightness of our lives?

Then this study of ourselves will enable us to discover the confusion of our operative psychology; we will perhaps find sins, or at least weaknesses, which call for repentance, for deep reform. We will see, for example, that certain outstanding characteristics of our personality are often anything but praise-worthy, particularly where our passions give us enjoyment of action, and therefore the illusion that we are free, whereas we are victims of ourselves, that is, of these blind instinctive ener-gies not worthy of a perfect man, far less of a follower of Christ.

—Papal audience, March 21, 1973

**The Spiritual Value of Work**   Yes, let us first honor work, from the subjective point of view, as a natural exigency of the human being. Man is a virtual, implicit being, in need of development and perfection.

This development and perfection do not come about in a due form and to a satisfactory extent by themselves, by vegetative growth, as it were; they come about by means of man's activity, a rational, orderly activity, which exercises human forces and faculties. This exercise is work.   —Papal audience, May 1, 1973

**Work Helps Us Fulfill Our Potential**   Man does not reach his real dimension without work, which is a binding, beneficial law for all of us. Woe betide idleness, laziness, waste of time, vain and superfluous use of one's capacities. Every man must be in some way an intelligent and willing worker.

Let us honor in work what makes it great, noble, deserving: duty. And let us recognize in work an inevitable and necessary program of our life; the right to work (cf. Gen 2:15; Mt 20:6).

—Papal audience, May 1, 1973

**Spiritual Values Must Permeate Human Development Efforts**
Enlightened by God's guidance, and uniquely rich in human experience, the Church knows and proclaims that the true advancement of man, the true progress of peoples, can be real-ized only when the spiritual values which answer their highest aspirations receive due emphasis.

And so the Church throughout the ages has communicated these values and promoted initiatives for the development of peoples, initiatives aimed at embracing every man and the whole man. The Church must then continue to affirm all the values of a truly human life, showing at the same time that our hearts are restless until they rest in God.

— World Communications Day, June 3, 1973

**The Little Way of St. Thérèse**   It is necessary to resume the practice of good, of honesty, seeking what is better in little things, that is, in the sequence of our ordinary actions, where our defects lie in wait for us at every moment, sometimes disastrously; and where, on the contrary, integrity of action can be easily perfected, if we remember the teaching of the Lord Jesus: "He who is faithful in a very little is faithful also in much" (Lk 16:10). This is something to begin with immediately, for everyone.                                 — Papal audience, June 20, 1973

**The Gift of Life**   It seems that the departure must be expressed in a great and simple act of recognition and gratitude. This mortal life is, not withstanding its labors, its hidden secrets, its sufferings, its fatal frailty, a most beautiful thing, a wonder ever original and moving, an event worthy to be celebrated in joy and glory: life, human life!

Not less worthy of exaltation and happy amazement is the framework in which human life is contained: this immense world, mysterious, magnificent; this universe with its thousand forces, thousand laws, thousand beauties, thousand depths.

Why have I not studied, explored, admired sufficiently this place in which life unfolds? What unpardonable distraction, what reprehensible superficiality!

However, even at the last we should recognize that this world, *qui per Ipsum factus est,* which was made through him, is amazing. With immense admiration, and as I have said, with gratitude I salute you and honor you at my leave-taking; behind life, behind nature and the universe, stands Wisdom, and there too, I will say it in these luminous last moments, stands Love.

This world's scene is the design, still today incomprehensible for the most part, of a Creator God, who calls himself our father in heaven. Thank you, O God, thanksgiving and glory to you, Father."          — Pope Paul VI's Testament, June 30, 1965, with additional notations on September 16, 1972, and July 14, 1973

# Conclusion

*Lectio divina* is an excellent model for processing Paul's human development teachings because of its holistic and developmental nature. We utilize our sensate, mental, emotional, and spiritual faculties when engaging in the activities of *lectio:* reading, meditation (reflection), prayer, contemplation (receptive presence before God), and action (implementation of the message received during *lectio*).

It is helpful to periodically refer to these faculties and activities as a potential fulfillment gauge. Am I utilizing my resources optimally during both *lectio divina* and life experiences?

Lest we be overwhelmed at the prospect of assimilating all this, we should remember that these are faculties and activities that we engage naturally in the process of reflecting prayerfully on a spiritual text. We don't have to proceed perfectly (whatever that is) or precisely (according to some predetermined regimen). Rather, we just have to be and apply ourselves in a sincere manner. *Lectio divina* is a framework rather than a straitjacket, and we should follow it accordance with our circumstances, capacities, and comfort level.

## Coach Paul

Like the Bible (cf. 1 Cor 9:24–27; 2 Tm 2:5), let's use an athletic analogy to convey important teachings. Athletes who practice diligently (which is analogous to reading and applying quality sources like Paul VI) and focus on controllable variables such as their efforts rather than on pressure-inducing external factors such as competition and referees usually perform to their capacity.

Paul is like a good coach:

◆ He assesses his players and the situation through study, discernment, and dialogue.

◆ He recognizes the strengths and tactics of the enemy (the world, the flesh, and the devil; cf. 1 Jn 2:16) and takes appropriate measures to counter and overcome them.

◆ He conveys the game plan through his teaching and adjusts it in response to developments — in his and Vatican II's terminology, by reading the signs of the times; cf. Mt 16:3.

◆ He balances instruction with freedom and trust so that his players are empowered to respond creatively, spontaneously, and resourcefully to their situation while remaining faithful to the game plan.

◆ He provides support through ongoing directives, encouragement, advocacy, and consolation.

◆ By linking the dignity and fortunes of the individual and community, he promotes teamwork (solidarity and cooperation).

Following are sample applications or components of the game plan:

◆ When I read Paul exhorting us to take our potential fulfillment seriously, I am reminded to periodically consider my purpose and direction in life and the way I utilize my capacities and resources. Do my values, habits, schedule, and lifestyle foster the realization of my and others' potential?

◆ When Paul explores the link between personal and communal development, I consider the extent to which I nurture my and others' spirituality and development and address areas in need of growth and healing.

◆ When Paul points out the role of justice and human dignity in authentic development, I consider whether I am living a life of integrity, which in the biblical languages means wholeness and justice, with Moses (cf. Nm 12:3; Dt 34:7), Job (cf. Job 1–2), the two Josephs (cf. Gen 37; Mt 1:19), and, of course, Jesus as good examples. Charity begins at home (cf. 1 Tm 5:4) and proceeds outward.

◆ Perhaps most compelling is the excerpt from Paul's testament that began this chapter. The questions he asks of himself I should likewise consider:

In what ways have I taken aspects of life for granted?

What superfluous distractions are diverting me from the richness and essential challenges of life? How might I change my direction and approach?

What superficialities are keeping me from exploring the breadth and depths of life?

In wrestling with these questions, I cannot help but engage my whole self in the foundational spiritual and developmental activities of *lectio divina*.

# Chapter 11

# Suffering

*As "an expert in humanity"... we feel we are making our own
the voice of the dead and of the living; of the dead, who fell in
the terrible wars of the past; of the living who survived those
wars, bearing in their hearts a condemnation of those who
would try to renew wars; and also of those living who rise up
fresh and confident, the youth of the present generation, who
legitimately dream of a better human race.*

*And we also make our own the voice of the poor, the
disinherited, the suffering, of those who hunger and thirst for
justice, for the dignity of life, for freedom, for well-being and
progress.*                                              —Pope Paul VI, Address to the
U.N. General Assembly, October 4, 1965

Many of Paul's admirers feel that he was a martyr for the Church.
He suffered enormously because of the middle path of compromise,
moderation, and reconciliation that he charted and the misunderstandings and disappointments that resulted. Extremists at both ends
of the ideological spectrum disliked him and sowed discontent:
progressives for his refusal to change Church teaching on contraception, priestly celibacy, and the exclusion of laity and women from
the priesthood, and traditionalists for his enthusiastic implementation of Vatican II reforms and forbearance with progressives and
dissidents.

St. Paul's letters to the Corinthians reveal that such contentiousness and rivalries are not new. Similar tensions continue today as
diverse interest groups strive to impose their vision and agenda on
the Church.

As discussed in the chapter on chastity, *Humanae Vitae* was the lightning rod of his pontificate and the source of much of his suffering. To this day it exemplifies the misunderstanding that surrounds Paul VI.

Restorationists (Catholics who wish to roll back the reforms of Vatican II) emphasize Paul's rejection of contraception while ignoring the nuances, evolving circumstances, and pastoral considerations that he acknowledged.

Progressives criticize his interpretation of and extensive reliance on the natural law in arriving at his decision and his rejection of collegiality (refusing to let the council fathers decide the issue) and the majority decision of the birth control commission. Neither side takes the encyclical in its entirety and context and wrestles with its balance between principle and pastoral sensitivity.

Rationalism, materialism, hedonism, and fundamentalism are all incapable of recognizing and maintaining in a healthy tension the objective and subjective dimensions of marriage and human sexuality. How tragic that a man such as Paul VI, who was able to consider all sides of an issue and come to a reasonable and balanced conclusion would be misunderstood on a subject in which his instincts served him and the Church so well.

The dissatisfaction with Paul did not stop there. Many didn't like the changes in the Mass and confession or the liberal laicization of priests and sisters. Clergy, religious, and laypersons were leaving the Church, or more precisely in most cases, their ministries, in significant numbers, and who was to blame other than Paul VI?

However, if you talk to priests from that era who remained, you will discover an appreciation of Paul's leniency and pastoral wisdom. They recognized the agony of their troubled peers and were grateful for Paul's compassionate approach. In some cases they have kept in touch with former colleagues who have found their niche as laypersons. They posed these questions: What purpose would it serve to deny a priest's request for laicization, presuming he has engaged in the prerequisite discernment and counsel? What kind of witness and minister would he be?

Instead of summarily silencing or ostracizing his vocal detractors, Paul reacted firmly but respectfully, responding to contentiousness with conciliation. When feasible he acted quietly and behind the scenes, seeking to preserve the dignity of those involved.

One of Paul's closest assistants, Monsignor Giovanni Benelli, whom Paul appointed cardinal and archbishop of Venice in June 1977, was particularly adept at executing Paul's wishes in an efficient and dignified manner. He was given serious consideration at the two 1978 papal conclaves.

Paul's quiet dignity and reluctance to air the Church's dirty laundry in public meant that we will never know all the details and rationales associated with his decisions and the events surrounding him. He was willing to be misunderstood rather than compromise himself, his position, or the dignity of others, the Church, and Catholic teaching. How rare and necessary such integrity and judiciousness is today. Am I willing to be misunderstood for the sake of the Gospel, the Church, and others?

Sensitive to the feelings and perspectives of others, Paul took these misunderstandings to heart, recognizing that he was imperfect and may have contributed to them. We can identify with this in light of our insecurities and weaknesses, particularly with respect to important decisions, communications, and relationships.

Reflection on Paul's plight leads inexorably to Jesus. The saints have often commented on the mental suffering of Jesus during both his passion and public ministry. He experienced the opposition of the religious leaders (whose knowledge of the Scriptures should have enlightened them as to his authenticity), the indifference and fickleness of the masses, the skepticism and possessiveness of his relatives, and the misguided energies and ambitions of his followers. He ate his last meal with his friends with the foreknowledge that one would betray him, one would deny him, and the rest would abandon him. He died misunderstood, rejected, and alone.

The more obvious forms of suffering such as physical and economic require little comment. We all have experience of them and know the insufficiency of words to describe them. However, in today's world where communication obstacles and breakdowns are so common it is important to consider the painful effects of misunderstanding and how we can let it become redemptive by uniting our suffering with the suffering of Jesus, Paul, and other believers, while trying to make others feel understood and accepted, particularly those closest to us and upon whom we have the greatest influence.

How ironic that an extraordinarily articulate diplomat with unparalleled cultural sensitivities (see the chapters on dialogue and evangelization) and a gift for making compelling gestures would end up being the most misunderstood pontiff of modern times.

One of Paul's original insights into Jesus' suffering was that because of his refined sensibilities, his experience of suffering would have been much more intense. This is dramatized in the agony in the garden.

Pope Paul shared with John Paul II an appreciation of St. Paul's inspiring assertion of the redemptive possibilities of suffering: "I am now rejoicing in my sufferings for your sake, and in my flesh I am completing what is lacking in Christ's afflictions for the sake of his body, that is, the church" (cf. Col 1:24). Both pontiffs made frequent reference to this in their addresses and letters. John Paul II began and ended his encyclical on suffering, *Salvifici Doloris,* by referencing this as a central aspect of Christian soteriology (the theology of salvation) and theodicy (the theology of suffering).

## SUFFERING

**The Message of the Cross**   The Christian message is not a prophecy of condemnation. It is a call to penance, because it is a call to salvation. . . . It is a message of strong and cheerful generosity, full of beauty and poetry, full of life and splendor. At the same time, it does raise the cross; the cross of sorrow, sacrifice, death; but in order to bring comfort, redemption, and life.
— Radio message for the mission of Milan, 1957

**The Utility of Suffering**   There is a saying which comes frequently to my mind. It belongs to St. Augustine and is, it seems to me, one of the most luminous left to us by this great genius who pronounces it with a sense of commiseration for those who do not know the wisdom of the Gospel and the sublime effect and value of suffering: "You have lost the sense of the utility

of suffering and you are become the most miserable of men." If
we men were to lose our sense of the value of toil, of pain, of
tears, of anguish and human death, what would it mean for us?
It would mean defeat!"

— Queen of Apostles Hospital, Albano, Italy, August 22, 1963

**The Horizons and Potentialities of Suffering**   In the light of
the Gospel, suffering acquires a meaning. . . . If it acquires value,
if it is worth something, it is not a matter of useless tears and a
pointless sacrifice.

What immense horizons, not only of spiritual life but of mystic and ascetical life, too, stretch before the man who views pain
from a Christian standpoint! He contemplates this crucifix (I saw
it dominating here over the altar) which says: "It was through
the ways of pain and sacrifice pushed to the point of death that
the world was saved, brought back, ransomed, and redeemed!"

— Queen of Apostles Hospital, Albano, Italy, August 22, 1963

**Various Responses to Suffering**   Behavior in suffering varies.
One can suffer with rebellion in his heart. The unbeliever, the
man who does not pray, suffers thus, even if he says nothing. How often, in passing through the words of the sick, one
hears, one sees this fearful silence — people who repress within
themselves a sense of despair, of rebellion, of unconsoled doubt.

There is a second form of suffering (I think it is also yours)
and it is that of patience. . . .

But there is another way (and it must be yours as loving
believers in Christ): to suffer *with love and for love* — not only
with patience, but also with love. And this can be done always,
even when there is no strength to say prayers or perform other
practices. As long as there is life, the heart is capable of loving —
this act so sublime, which sums up our whole spirituality. "Lord,
I weep, I suffer, I lie here inert and immobile, but I love You, and
I suffer for Love, for You!"

From this it can be seen that our actions acquire value
through the thought which accompanies them, that is, through
the intention which ennobles them.

— Queen of Apostles Hospital, Albano, Italy, August 22, 1963

**Various Intentions in Suffering**    Oh, for how many intentions! ...For we know that one intention does not exclude another. There can be a whole ladder of intentions. I can suffer in order to obey my rules, to give good example, to mortify myself, to be similar to Christ, and I can do it also (stupendous mystery of the redemption!) to transcend my very spirituality and pass over the bounds of my personal destiny, saying: "I suffer for poor sinners, for the missions, for the council, for the Church, for my religious family...for many who suffer badly...for children...for the good press, for the Pope."

You, who suffer silently and pray, you who love, can do much good to the holy Church of God through the sanctification and sublimation of these dark days of suffering through which you are now passing.

— Queen of Apostles Hospital, Albano, Italy, August 22, 1963

**A Modern Beatitude**    We are blessed if we prefer to be oppressed rather than oppressors, if we know how to pardon and to fight, to work and to serve, to suffer and to love.

— Papal audience, January 5, 1964

**When I Was in Prison**    Let me tell you that I have come here because of my affection for you and that my sympathy for you knows no limits.

If you are ever struck sad by the thought that nobody is fond of you, that everyone looks on you with a gaze which humiliates and mortifies you, that society which has sent you here condemns you, that perhaps even your own relatives regard you with insistent reproach for what you have done, well then, just remember that I, in coming here, consider you with deep understanding and great esteem.

— To the inmates of Regina Coeli, a Roman jail, April 9, 1964

**Union with Christ through Suffering**    To all of you, brothers in trial, who are visited by suffering under a thousand forms, the council has a very special message. It feels on itself your pleading eyes, burning with fever or hollow with fatigue, questioning eyes which search in vain for the why of human suffering and which ask anxiously when and whence will come relief.

Very dear brothers, we feel echoing deeply within our hearts as fathers and pastors your laments and your complaints. Our suffering is increased at the thought that it is not within our power to bring you bodily help nor the lessening of your physical sufferings, which physicians, nurses and all those dedicated to the service of the sick are endeavoring to relieve as best they can.

But we have something deeper and more valuable to give you, the only truth capable of answering the mystery of suffering and of bringing you relief without illusion, and that is faith and union with the Man of Sorrows, with Christ the Son of God, nailed to the cross for our sins and for our salvation.

— Closing session, Vatican Council II, December 7, 1965

**Becoming Christ's Image through Suffering**   Christ did not do away with suffering. He did not even wish to unveil to us entirely the mystery of suffering. He took suffering upon Himself and this is enough to make you understand all its value.

All of you who feel heavily the weight of the cross, you who are poor and abandoned, you who weep, you who are persecuted for justice, you who are ignored, you the unknown victims of suffering, take courage. You are the preferred children of the kingdom of God, the kingdom of hope, happiness and life. You are the brothers of the suffering Christ, and with Him, if you wish, you are saving the world.

This is the Christian science of suffering, the only one which gives peace. Know that you are not alone, separated, abandoned or useless. You have been called by Christ and are His living and transparent image.

— Closing session, Vatican Council II, December 7, 1965

**The Efficacious Prayers of Sufferers**   We would point out that We rely particularly on the prayers of the innocent and the suffering, for their voices more than any others reach Heaven and disarm God's justice.

— Closing session, Vatican Council II, December 7, 1965

**Uniting Our Suffering with Christ's**   Those members of the Church who are stricken by infirmities, illnesses, poverty or misfortunes, or who are persecuted for the love of justice, are invited to unite their sorrows to the suffering of Christ in such a way that they not only satisfy more thoroughly the precept of penitence but also obtain for the brethren a life of grace and for themselves that beatitude which is promised in the Gospel to those who suffer.   —*Apostolic Constitution on Fast and Abstinence,* February 17, 1966

**The Lord's Prophecy of Suffering for His Followers**   We well remember that profession of the Christian faith naturally entails a drama (because it is different from the world and against its corrupting seductions and "pomps," as the rite of baptism used to say, until yesterday). It entails a disadvantage, a risk, an effort, a "martyrdom" that is, a hard act of testimony and a sacrifice. The Lord told his followers: "If they persecuted me, they will persecute you..." (Jn 15:20); "...the world will rejoice; you will be sorrowful, but your sorrow will turn into joy" (Jn 16:20). I came, he said, not to bring cowardly peace at any price, but the sword of moral courage (cf. Mt 10:34). He is a "target for contradiction" (Lk 2:34). Anyone who wishes to follow him will have to carry his own cross (Mt 10:38).

—Papal audience, April 29, 1970

**Acute Suffering in the Religious Life**   It was along this way that Therese Couderc mainly showed that she was a saint, if sanctity is truly formed and truly manifests itself through the cross. She bore it for forty-five years. That cross is such that the religious life weighs upon the person who takes it up, sometimes in a particularly heavy and strange manner upon anyone who has the grace of being a founder. A Foundress's mission can become painfully dramatic in certain circumstances, especially when the difficulties come from those in authority in the Church and from those who share the lot of community life; in other words, when the person who causes suffering is venerated and good, and has a paternal relationship or that of spiritual filiation to the sufferer.

This is a kind of suffering which we would not suppose to be possible at first sight, indeed we would not even imagine it to exist. It occurs in relation with ties established in the field of ecclesial charity, the most demanding and finest of the things the Lord left us. It is for this very reason that every wound inflicted upon such relationships produces the most acute pain.

—Papal audience, May 10, 1970

**Intimacy Exacerbates Suffering**   Love increases sensitivity, and transmits feeling from the exterior to the heart. But we are human beings, which means that we are capable of making our fellow men suffer, those nearest and dearest to us above all, and even with the best intentions. If our defects aggravate the wrong in the injury we do and make it offensive, bitterness sinks deeply in, and causes reactions such as only superior virtue can contain.                                     —Papal audience, May 10, 1970

**Christ's Daunting Foreknowledge**   We cannot disregard, in the first place, the tragic end of Christ's earthly life, the drama of his death on the cross. Nor can we overlook an extraordinary fact, which gives exceptional significance to this drama: Jesus knew that he would die in this way. No hero knows the fate that awaits him. No mortal can measure the time he still has to live, or know how much and what suffering he will have to bear.

But Jesus did know. Can we imagine the psychology of a man who clearly foresees a moral and physical martyrdom, such as Jesus bore? On several occasion, at moments of complete awareness, he foretold his passion to his disciples. The Gospel narrative is full of these prophetic confidences, which show Jesus's heart-rending foreknowledge of the fate that awaited him (cf. Mk 8:3; 9:31; 10:33ff.). He knew "his hour"; this matter of "his hour" would be an extremely interesting meditation to penetrate a little into Christ's mind.

The evangelist John dedicates frequent precious indications to it (cf. Jn 2:4; 7:30; 12:23; 13:1; 17:1). Christ, one would think has continually in front of him the clock of future time, and of present time in reference to the mysterious cycles of events seen by God. The prophecies of the past and those of the future are an open book before his divine eye (cf. Gospel of St. Matthew; Jn 13:18; 15:25; Lk 24:25; etc).

—Papal audience, February 17, 1971

**The Man for Others**   And we can point out some distinctive features of his moral figure, of his heart; Jesus was kind with a divine kindness (cf. Mk 10:17, 19, 21); he had understanding of other people's pain and distress (Mt 11:18); he was able to comprehend, forgive and rehabilitate; his meetings with sinners are well known. Jesus has been magnificently understood and defined, in contemporary Christological discussion, as "the man for others." That's it. And St. Paul, that is, all the theology of the New Testament and of Catholic Tradition, had a deep insight into the secret of Christ's earthly life, the reason, the purpose of the Incarnation, and tells us in what form and to what extent Jesus was for others: "Jesus died for our sins in accordance with the Scriptures" (1 Cor 15:3)       —Papal audience, February 17, 1971

**Remembering the Pain of Christ**   Jesus offers himself for us and to us as He was on the cross, immolated, tormented, consumed in pain carried to its highest degree of physical sensibility and spiritual desolation.

Remember his very human pangs: "I am thirsty!" (Jn 19:28); and his unutterable torments: "My God! My God! Why have you deserted me?" (Mt 27:46), do you remember?

—Mass for Invalids from Roman Hospitals on the Feast of Corpus Domini, June 10, 1971

**Providence in Pain**   Furthermore God, in a miracle of his Providence, conferred on pain a utility of its own, supreme in the economy of the cross and of Redemption, and allowed man to recover good, and often a good of a higher nature, in every condition of ours, however wretched and unfavorable it may be. "We know that in everything God works for good with those who love him," St. Paul says (Rom 8:28).

—Papal audience, February 7, 1973

**The Spirit Does Not Remove the Cross**   The coming of the Holy Spirit does not take the cross away from human reality. It is not a charm, making human life immune to suffering and misfortune. It is not a preventive medicine, an insurance, a physical therapy against the ills of our present existence "Non pacem sed gladium" (I have not come to bring peace, but a sword — Mt 10:34).

In fact, there seems to be a secret sympathy between grace and human suffering. Why? The Lord taught us the reason with many weighty words that leave no doubt. With regard to himself, in the first place, he admonished the sorrowing travelers on the way to Emmaus. "Was it not necessary that the Christ should suffer these things and enter into his glory?" (Lk 24:26).

— Papal audience, June 26, 1974

**The Normality of Suffering in the Life of the Disciple**   What would be left of the Gospel without the Passion and death of Jesus? And is it possible to visualize the Church, which is his living continuation, without participation in the drama of his suffering?

"I say to you" he declared at the Last Supper, "That you will weep and lament, but the world will rejoice" (Jn 16:20). He had said this several times in different words. "He who does not take up his cross and follow me is not worthy of me" (Mt 10:38, 16–24). Indeed are not the Apostles of the same school? St. Paul's words are famous. "I rejoice now in the sufferings I bear for your sake; and what is lacking in the sufferings of Christ I fill up in my flesh for his body, which is the Church" (Col 1:24).

There would be no end if we wished to make an anthology of the teachings of Scripture on the necessity (Acts 5:41), the "normality," we could say, of suffering in the life Christ's follower.

— Papal audience, June 26, 1974

**God Can Redeem Every Human Situation**   We must seek the first comforting thought in the existence and goodness of God. He leaves to human vicissitudes the sinister developments that may derive from the capricious, unstable and fallible freedom, which the economy of the superior government of the world grants to that tiny, but terrible being, called man.

The latter, because of his shortcomings or because of his malice, (with the complicity of another mysterious and evil being, the devil!), can upset the ideal and regular development of man's own activity. But this disorder does not immobilize the hand of God, who can intervene and can draw a new good from the evil caused by the wickedness of his creature.

In fact this operation of restoring order is another great effect of divine presence on the human scene, a presence which can draw positive effects from every human situation. Let us recall St. Paul, who assures us that "God works for good with those who love him" (Rom 8:28).

—First audience after the assassination of former Italian prime minister Aldo Moro, May 17, 1978

**The Consoling Role of Providence amid Suffering** One of the arts of divine Providence in our regard is precisely that of making us find treasures of salvation in the very experience of certain evils which cause suffering in our lives. Here let us recall the immensely consoling, innovating words of Christ himself: "Blessed are those who mourn, for they shall be comforted" (Mt 5:4). They are echoed by another expression of the Divine Master, concerning the tribulations of the last period of history: "By your endurance you will gain your lives" (Lk 21:19).

—First audience after the assassination of former Italian prime minister Aldo Moro, May 17, 1978

**Consolation in Suffering** There is in human suffering a certainty which should ease it and make it tolerable. It is that suffering is not useless: it is connected, which made St. Francis of Assisi, though afflicted by his stigmata, say: "So great is the joy which I await, that all suffering is dear to me."

Among the great marvels effected by Christianity there is also that of having taught people to suffer patiently and to discover treasures of humanity and grace in pain and misfortune.

—First audience after the assassination of former Italian prime minister Aldo Moro, May 17, 1978

## Conclusion

*Lectio divina* is an ideal model for dealing with suffering because it is holistic and encourages candid communications. I continually experience this not only in my own life, but when presenting workshops in health-care and support group environments. I developed a program entitled *Job Therapy* that utilizes *lectio divina* in conjunction with the book of Job and related guided imagery in order to help persons cope with suffering and care-giving.

Paul's words on suffering are ideal for *lectio* because they are compassionate, consoling, and drawn from experience. Unlike Job's friends, Paul knows better than to engage in platitudes or insensitive, simplistic statements that deepen the isolation and emotional and spiritual turmoil that accompanies suffering. He recognizes the harsh realities of suffering and interprets them in light of the message and model of Jesus and New Testament epistle exhortations. The letters of Paul, Peter, James, and Hebrews contain multiple acknowledgments of the pervasive presence and the redemptive potential of suffering.

With respect to counsel on suffering, less is often more. Given Paul's pithy poignancy and *lectio*'s capacity for extracting much from a small amount of text, we should be particularly vigilant about biting off a manageable chunk of text and giving it and the Spirit sufficient time to penetrate our hearts and enlighten us to personal applications and meaning. The guidance and consolation we receive can then heal and transform us according to the ways and timetable of nature and providence.

# Chapter 12

# Humility

*Men cannot be brothers if they are not humble. It is pride, no matter how legitimate it may seem to be, which provokes tension and struggles for prestige, for predominance, colonialism, egoism; that is, pride disrupts brotherhood.*

*In fact, we have nothing to ask for, no question to raise; we have only a desire to express and a permission to request; namely, that of serving you insofar as we can, with disinterest, with humility and love.*                   —Pope Paul VI, Address to the
U.N. General Assembly, October 4, 1965

Paul VI was a very unassuming person. He did not enjoy crowds and did not project well before large audiences. He was charismatic and engaging in person but not in public.

Paul's humility was accompanied by patience and forbearance. He did not respond rashly or vindictively to those who questioned or opposed his policies. He chose to dialogue with them rather than impose his authority capriciously. His detractors viewed him as vacillating and timid.

The early seventies was a period of shakeout in the Church. The Vatican II reforms had been going on for half a decade, and the revised rite of the liturgy had recently been put in place (1969). The new rite was one of the greatest achievements of Paul's pontificate. The architect of the rite, Monsignor Annibale Bugnini, published a fascinating 976-page book entitled *The Reform of the Liturgy* (Liturgical Press, 1990), in which he documented the development of the new rite.

Paul VI's humility served him and the Church well in letting the implementation of Vatican II run its course. Decentralization and subsidiarity led to a renewal at every level of the Church (bureaucratic, diocesan, pastoral, and familial). Certainly there were excesses, and in many cases seemingly avoidable ones, but Paul refused to indiscriminately "crack down" on innovators and thereby obstruct progress and dialogue. He chose to use his authority in a prudent, discrete, and gentle manner and rein in excesses through persuasion and correction rather than coercion.

As powerful as Paul's words of humility were, his gestures were even more so. He divested himself and the papacy of many of its medieval trappings. He reformed and streamlined the Curia (the Vatican bureaucracy), gave away the papal tiara (it is on display along with other mementos of Vatican II and Paul's trip to New York City in the basement of the Basilica Shrine of the Immaculate Conception in Washington, D.C.), enhanced ecumenical relations by his warm initiatives and demeanor, and planned a nonostentatious funeral. His last will and testament, excerpted at the conclusion of the Human Development chapter, was a humble and joyful reflection on life highlighted by this poignant observation: "Why have I not studied, explored, admired sufficiently this place in which life unfolds? What unpardonable distraction, what reprehensible superficiality!"

Am I willing to emulate Paul VI in subordinating my ego and seeking the Lord's will rather than mine? Am I willing to exercise patience, charity, and forbearance with those who trouble me? Am I willing to accept my and others' limitations and weaknesses and work with God and others to make the best of them? Let us humbly join Paul in thought, prayer, and action in seeking first the kingdom of God and allowing God to prune us of whatever inhibits its progress.

## *HUMILITY*

**Poverty of Spirit**   The third way [of poverty] is the most important and the most difficult for us to practice: poverty of spirit, the detachment of the heart from the overwhelming and tangled chains which bind us to the riches and values of the world.
— Christmas, 1959

**Proper Use of Temporal Goods**   Wealth owes its value to the service it renders man; but if man does not use it with a heart that is strong and free, that is, in a spirit of poverty, it becomes the master and he the servant. . . .

Simplicity, frugality, liberality in the use of temporal goods, these are signs of a spirit which can rise above them.

— Holy Week, 1963

**Following Jesus' Beatitudinal Example**  He taught us the way of the beatitudes of the Gospel: poverty in spirit, meekness, suffering borne with patience, thirst after justice, mercy, purity of heart, will for peace, persecution suffered for justice' sake.

— "Credo" of the People of God, July 30, 1968

**Poverty and Salvation**  The whole message of salvation emits an exhortation to Poverty, which shows us a divine intention penetrating the whole system of the supernatural relations established by revelation between God and man: God's salvific plan is addressed to men detached from earthly goods; Poverty is a constitutional element in the plan of Christian religion.

— Papal audience, October 2, 1968

**Cultural and Human Aversion to Poverty**  The necessity of economic goods is imposed by human nature itself, which needs bread (cf. Mt 6:11; Lk 11:3; Mt 6:32); and by the duty of trading talents (Mt 25:15); and of supplying others with the means of living and prospering (cf. Mt 20:6). . . .

The whole of modern life, dominated by temporal aims, and especially by economic ones, concerned with production, distribution, the enjoyment of earthly goods, seems to be focused on wealth, on sociology for or against capitalism, that is, on a conception contrary to Poverty, to which our Christian vocation calls us more urgently today. How can we cope with this fundamental difficulty?         — Papal audience, October 2, 1968

**Christian Poverty, Whether We Like It or Not**  The poverty of Christ, whether one likes it or not, is essentially a liberation, an invitation to a new and higher life, where the goods of the spirit, not earthly goods, have supremacy, which for some people — the perfect followers (cf. Mk 10:21) — becomes exclusive, for others hierarchical (cf. Mt 6:33); it is the best condition to enter the kingdom of God (cf. Mt 5:3); it is the initiation not to want, not to lack of understanding for the world that sweats and works, that builds and progresses, but to love.

To love, it is necessary to give; to give, it is necessary to be freed of selfishness, to have the courage of Poverty.

— Papal audience, October 2, 1968

**Poverty of Spirit Is Fundamental to Christianity**   The example of the Lord is summed up in a concise sentence of St. Paul's: "Though he (Jesus Christ) was rich, yet for your sake he became poor, so that by his poverty you might become rich (2 Cor 8:9).

The whole message of salvation outlines an exhortation to poverty, which shows us a divine intention penetrating the whole system of supernatural relations established by revelation between God and man. God's salvific plan is addressed to men detached from earthly goods; poverty is a constitutional element in the design of the Christian religion.

— Papal audience, October 2, 1968

**Simplicity and Humility Preserve Logic**   In fact simple souls, children, humble people, the pure of heart particularly have a healthier and more convincing natural logic than those who in the development of their reason have violated, or forgotten, certain of its exigencies.        — Papal audience, November 27, 1968

**The Eternal Value of Works**   Works accomplished in this life keep their value in the other: Opera enim illorum sequantur illos, the Apocalypse says of those who have died in the Lord (Rev 14:13). But those works affect those in heaven. In heaven they are splendor and joy. But on earth, how do they appear, what are they like?

The perennial Gospel of the Beatitudes tells us in its dramatic way; here below sanctity is poverty, humility, suffering sacrifice, that is imitation of Christ, the Word of God made man; imitation of him in his kenosis, his twofold humiliation in the Incarnation and in the Redemption.        — Papal audience, January 25, 1970

**The Need for Renunciation**    One of the least understood, and we could say least popular, aspects of Christian life for us moderns, is renunciation. We are so stimulated by the variety and the quantity of all the things available today for a comfortable life, rich in experiences, full and happy, that it seems to us absurd to renounce anything, particularly if the renunciation concerns the training, education, culture and welfare of man.

—Papal audience, March 11, 1970

**The Meaning of Sacrifice**    Christian renunciation is not the arbitrary, burdensome, ascetic and monastic discipline of the past. It is an authentic way of Christian life.

Firstly, because it implies a hierarchical classification of its goods; secondly, because it stimulates us to choose the "better part" (Lk 10:42); thirdly, because it gives man practice in self-control; lastly, because it establishes that mysterious economy of expiation, which makes us participants in Christ's redemption.

A word which in everyday language now refers to renunciation, reminds us of this: the word "sacrifice." In itself it takes us back to a mysterious and supreme act of religion, but which now, in the sign of that cross, bringing death and life at the same time, indicates a generous and courageous act, a joyful and voluntary renunciation, carried out with a higher intention of good and of love.

Sacrifice: a strong word, which derives from the first "little sacrifices" of the child, who really wants to be good, and spreads over all ages and in various measures, to detach us from the many "useless and harmful desires" (1 Tm 6:9), and to qualify us to give our earthly existence the significance and the value of "a sacrifice, living, holy, pleasing to God" (Rom 12:1).

—Papal audience, March 11, 1970

**Evangelical Poverty**    The fact is that evangelical poverty entails a corrective to our religious relationship with God and Christ. The reason is that this relationship creates a prior claim. That claim is for spiritual goods to be first in the list of values worthy of being put in the forefront of our existence, our seeking and our love. That claim is expressed in the command: Seek you first the kingdom of God" (Mt 6:33).

Then (this is what poverty is!) it puts temporal goods, wealth, present happiness, low down on the list in comparison with the supreme good, which is God and in comparison with the possession of him, which is our everlasting happiness.

Humbleness of heart, temperance, and, often, detachment in regard to possession and use of economic goods, are the two marks of poverty which the divine Master taught us with his doctrine — and even more by his example, as We said. He revealed himself socially through poverty.

—Papal audience, June 24, 1970

**Poverty of Spirit Is a Choice and Lifestyle**   We can at once see that this theological principle upon which Christian poverty is based turns into a moral principle, and this moral principle inspires Christian asceticism. According to it, poverty is more than a mere fact for man. It is the willed result of a love preference, a choice of Christ and his realm, together with renunciation (which is a liberation) of covetousness, of riches. Desire for riches entails a whole series of temporal cares and earthly ties which occupy great and overwhelming space in the heart.

Let us not forget the Gospel story of the rich young man. He was given the chance of following Christ and therefore abandoning his riches. He preferred his wealth to the following of Christ. The Lord "looked upon him and loved him" (Mt 10:21), but still had to watch him go sadly away.      —Papal audience, June 24, 1970

**Material Means and Spiritual Ends**   There is need for economic and material means. That entails the necessity to look for means, to ask for them, to administer them. But may those "means" never get the better of the concept of the "ends" which they ought to serve. The means ought to reflect the restraint created by the limits of the ends, the generosity of commitment to them, and the spirituality of their significance.

In the Divine Master's school we shall all remember to love poverty and the poor at the same time. We shall love the former in order to make it an austere norm of Christian life. We shall love the latter in order to devote special interest to them, whether they be persons, classes or nations in need of love and aid. —Papal audience, June 24, 1970

## *Conclusion*

Humility and poverty of spirit, the attitude of waiting on God characteristic of the Old Testament *anawim* (poor of Yahweh), is innate to a proper practice of *lectio divina*.

One of the characteristics of the *anawim* is that they are either silent or direct in their communications. The lament psalms reflect the spirit of the *anawim,* and given the tendency of suffering persons to go on and on about their pain (e.g., Job and Jeremiah), they are remarkably terse. In most cases we don't know the precise affliction, trial, or misfortune that they are lamenting. A seventeenth-century spiritual classic containing the teachings of Jean-Pierre de Caussade, S.J. entitled *Self-Abandonment to Divine Providence* anticipates the Little Way of the Little Flower, St. Thérèse of Lisieux, and captures this *anawim* spirit. Their reflections complement Paul's and are helpful for cultivating the *anawim* disposition.

*Lectio* helps us assimilate the *anawim* mentality of fidelity to God's will and humble trust in providence. United with Paul in recognition of our absolute dependence on God, we can reflect on his exposition of the efficacy of humility and poverty of spirit and pray for the strength to practice it in accordance with God's will.

# Chapter 13

# Joy

*As long as man remains that weak, changeable and even wicked being that he often shows himself to be, defensive arms will, unfortunately, be necessary. You, however, in your courage and valiance, are studying the ways of guaranteeing the security of international life, without having recourse to arms. This is a most noble aim. . . .*

*Gratitude will be expressed to you by all peoples, relieved as they will then be from the crushing expenses of armaments and freed from the nightmare of an ever imminent war.*

*We rejoice in the knowledge that many of you have considered favorably our invitation, addressed to all states in the cause of peace from Bombay last December, to divert to the benefit of the developing countries at least a part of the savings which could be realized by reducing armaments.*

—Pope Paul VI, Address to the
U.N. General Assembly, October 4, 1965

Popes do not frequently compose apostolic letters or encyclicals on a general spiritual topic such as joy. Usually these letters address contemporary topics of theology, discipline (Church order and practice), social justice, or morality, particularly controversial ones. Recent exceptions to this include Paul VI's *Gaudete in Domino* ("On Christian Joy") and John Paul II's *Salvifici Doloris* ("On the Christian Meaning of Human Suffering").

In 1975, Paul VI was nearing the end of a lengthy and turbulent pontificate. He was discouraged by the spread of secularism in both society and the Church, and the resistance to and distorted implementations of Vatican II reforms. A banking scandal had shaken the

176

Vatican, and the pope had long since abandoned international trips. Paul was in the home stretch, and few initiatives were expected.

In May 1975, Paul surprised the Church by issuing an apostolic exhortation on Christian joy. This was particularly unexpected from a pope who did not project the joviality of John XXIII and whose writings and addresses were intellectual and sober.

However, this disparity fades when one considers the joy manifested in Paul's private persona, personal relationships, and spirituality. Paul had a playful, humorous side. He came off as serious due to his public shyness, humility, the magnitude of his responsibilities, and the issues facing him.

The paradox of joy in Paul's life is instructive for us. The opening words of his apostolic letter *Gaudete in Domino*, "Rejoice in the Lord," identify the source and reason for his attitude. Like other gifts of the Spirit such as peace, fortitude, and wisdom, spiritual joy is not rooted in feelings or favorable situations. It is not transitory or dependent on external factors. It cannot be equated with pleasure or fleeting feelings of happiness or ecstasy. It is not bliss. We cannot experience perfect joy in this life, but we can get a foretaste.

Spiritual joy is very much like the peace received from God and beyond all understanding identified by St. Paul in Phil 4:7. It is not dependent upon willpower, circumstances, or emotions, but on faith in the crucified and risen Lord. Paradoxically and mysteriously, our joy is rooted in the Lord's death and our participation in it through our suffering and death.

Many of the selections in this section are not from *Gaudete in Domino*. Spiritual joy was a frequent theme of Pope Paul. Most important, he exemplified it. It helped him persevere and provide peerless guidance, inspiration, and leadership during one of the most turbulent periods in both world and church history.

Paul's joyfulness is particularly helpful in our pleasure-seeking yet joy-starved times. It reminds us that our fulfillment is not to be found exclusively in earthly realities. It is not something outside of us, over which we have no control. We can't manufacture, force, or merit it. It is a gift of the Spirit bestowed gratuitously by God upon those who will receive it.

As Paul frequently reminds us, we have to be properly disposed to receive and spread joy. Our attitudes, lifestyle, and actions must be in synch with Christian principles and morals and open to divine guidance.

Spiritual gifts are rooted in divine and human freedom. I can seek joy, carnal pleasures, or neither. As I read Paul's reflections, I periodically consider whether I am properly disposed to the joy offered by the Lord. Do I live in a way that enables me to recognize and receive it? If my heart and priorities are elsewhere, I will not desire or accept such joy. What do I want? Pope Paul's words can help me discern my state of mind and heart and what I can do to be a better receptacle and messenger of such joy. Let us join Paul on this joyful journey.

## *JOY*

**Joy Is a Christian Staple**   The Christian life is not without joy. In it we will find other elements besides joy — it includes the cross, renunciation, mortification, penitence, pain and sacrifice. But it never lacks a deep consolation, a sense of joy, which should never be lost, and is never lost when our souls are in God's grace.

When God is with us can we be altogether sad, bitter, desperate? No, the joy of God must always be, at least basically, a prerogative of the Christian soul.      —Papal audience, April 18, 1968

**Serene and Secure in Christ**   We Christians should not feel unhappier than other people because we have accepted Christ's yoke — a yoke that he bears with us and which he describes as "light" and "easy." On the contrary, we should feel happier than others, because we have splendid and secure reasons to be happier.

We are better placed than others who lack the light of the Gospels, to view with happy wonder the panorama of life and the world. We can enjoy with grateful serenity whatever life has in store for us, even its frequent trials.

The Christian is lucky. He knows how to find proofs of the goodness of God in every event, in every aspect of history and experience. He knows that "all things work together for good to them that love God."

The Christian must always show forth his greater security, so that others may see whence he derives his serene spiritual superiority — from the joy of Christ.

—Papal audience, April 17, 1968

**Christ Is the Reason for Our Joy**   Today this attitude, revealing a happy strength of spirit, is fortunately spreading among Christians. They are more self-possessed, more cheerful than formerly; and this is a good thing.

But it is good only on condition that they do not fall into a gay naturalism, which can easily become pagan and illusory. Their joy and serenity must derive from faith, not from fortunate worldly circumstances. Christ is our happiness. Let us repeat in his honor, and for our comfort: Alleluia!

—Papal audience, April 17, 1968

**Reciprocating the Creator's Joy**   And to our mind, to us who are in the school of faith, come the words of Holy Scripture "God created the heavens and the earth.... And God saw that it was good... God saw all he had made, and indeed it was very good" (Gen 1:21–31). This joy God experienced in the presence of his creatures, why should we not have this same joy toward our Creator?

—Papal audience, April 4, 1970

**A Time to Rejoice**   Alleluia! We would like all of you to enjoy this moment of spiritual happiness, and to understand its truth, its uniqueness, its depth; to be here, Alleluia!

Rare are the moments in which one can be happy without limits, without fears, without remorse! Remember the verses of the psalm: "I was glad when they said to me, 'Let us go to the house of the Lord!'" (Ps 121).

Religion, faith, grace have these moments of inner exultation, these surprises of the Spirit, these sweet, impetuous preludes of God's life in us. Yes, Alleluia, in Christ and in the Church. "Joy, joy, tears of joy" (Pascal).

—Papal audience, April 25, 1970

**The Gift of Joy**    The joy of a moment of plenitude, both sensible and spiritual, is not sufficient; joy must be perennial, even if of a lower degree of intensity. The believer, he who has succeeded in meeting the risen Christ, even though in the incognito of our earthly pilgrimage (cf. Lk 24:32), should always have within him the charism of joy. Joy, with peace, is the first fruit of the Spirit (Gal 5:22).          —Papal audience, April 25, 1970

**The Sermon on the Mount: Program for the Kingdom**    The Sermon on the Mount — in which the poor, the meek, and the pure, those who mourn, those who thirst for justice and the persecuted are called happy — is made by him into the program of a new kingdom, a kingdom whose symbol is the great emblem of the cross, and which is founded on the law of dying in order to live, that is, of duty and of sacrifice.    —Christmas Message, 1970

**Happiness Is Not Found in Possessions**    Perhaps never before has the world had such need of spiritual values, and, we are convinced, never has it been so disposed to welcome their proclamation. For the most affluent regions of the world are fast discovering for themselves that happiness does not consist in possessions; they are learning from a bitter "emptiness of experience" how true are our Lord's words: "Not on bread alone does man live, but on every word that proceeds from the mouth of God" (Mt 4:4).          —Mission Sunday, June 25, 1971

**Welcoming Jesus**    Brothers and sisters! Christ has come — he who today is our Savior, but tomorrow our Judge. Let us not reject him. Let us not ignore him. Like the shepherds after the announcement, let us say to ourselves: "Let us go to see what has happened" (cf. Lk 2:15).

Let us open to him, to Christ, the door of our consciousness, of our personal, family and social life. He does not come to take away, but to give! He does not come to obstruct our freedom, our activity, or our humanity. He comes to enlighten, enlarge and gladden this life of ours which, if we consider it, really needs in every respect this mysterious infant guest, Jesus.

          —Christmas Message, 1971

**Easter Is a Season and Attitude of Joy**    Anyone who has realized that the first consequence of Christian life is personal, interior to the person himself, cannot celebrate Easter, as we are invited to do so by the Church, merely on Easter Sunday; but also in the period following the feast, he cannot but feel that this consequence has a dominant psychological expression of its own, which is joy.

Before joy, we know, there is grace and with grace, peace; but the latter, in itself, passes our interior sensibility (cf. Phil 4:7), although it diffuses in the whole human being a certain ineffable well-being, a balance, a vigor, a confidence, a "spirit," which gives the soul a new sense of itself, of life and of things.

But joy is, more than any other spiritual fruit stemming from grace, from charity, its dominant effect (Gal 5:22), so much so that joy pervades the paschal liturgy, with its "alleluia" and with all the wave of gaiety marking the style Christian life at this season.                                          —Papal audience, April 19, 1972

**Joy Should Characterize Our Lives**    We discover, in fact, in celebrating the paschal mystery, that joy spreads throughout the Christian life beyond all calendar limits; it is its atmosphere, its characteristic note. Remember the exhortation of the Apostle Paul: "Rejoice in the Lord always; again I will say, Rejoice!" (Phil 4:4; 3:1).                                          —Papal audience, April 19, 1972

**Reconciling Suffering and Joy through the Paschal Mystery**
But here a difficulty arises. Is not the cross a sign of the Christian? Is not the sadness of repentance as normal and binding as the joy irradiating from the vital newness of the resurrection? To honor it, tolerate it, exploit it by merging it with the Lord's passion (cf. Col 1:24).

And then, do not all the so-called passive virtues, such as humility, patience, obedience, forgiveness of wrongs, service of one's brothers, etc., do they not stamp on the Christian countenance the stigmata of his real nature? And is not sacrifice the peak-point of Christian greatness? Where then is joy? How are we to reconcile these two opposite expressions of Christian life, suffering and joy?

The question is spontaneous and the answer is not easy. Let us look for it first of all in the drama of the paschal mystery itself, that is, redemption, which realizes in Christ the synthesis of justice and mercy, expiation and atonement, death and life.

Sorrow and joy are no longer irreducible enemies. The supreme law of dying in order to live is the key to understanding Christ the priest and victim (cf. Jn 12:14–15), that is, in his essential definition as Savior.                    — Papal audience, April 19, 1972

**The Sacraments Reconcile Joy and Sorrow**    Let us look for the answer to the problem of the harmony between joy and sorrow in Christian life in the sacramental application of Christ's salvation to our individual personal existences, in baptism and in the Eucharist particularly. Let us look for it in the succession of the different phases in which the pattern of our present life is divided.

Is not the evangelical message of the beatitudes the revelation of a connection between an unhappy, poor, mortified, oppressed present, and a future of bliss, recovery and fullness? Blessed, in a future tomorrow (of which they have a foretaste now) will be those who today are poor, weeping, oppressed... Jesus proclaims.

The solution revolves around hope, and in Christ "hope does not disappoint us" (Rom 5:5), "You will weep and lament, but the world will rejoice; you will be sorrowful, but your sorrow will turn into joy," Jesus says again (Jn 16:20).

                                                — Papal audience, April 19, 1972

**Joy and Sorrow Can Live Together**    In fact, on careful consideration we see that in the faithful experience of Christian life the two moments, that of suffering and that of joy, can be superimposed and become simultaneous, at least to a partial extent. St. Paul says so in a vivid sentence: "With all our affliction, I am overjoyed" (2 Cor 7:4). Joy and sorrow can live together.

This is one of the highest, most interesting and complex points of the psychology of the Christian, as if he lived, as he actually does, a double life; his own human, earthly life, subject to a thousand adversities, and Christ's life, which has already been infused into him, initially but really. "It is no longer I who live, the Apostle says further, but Christ who lives in me" (Gal 2:20). And Christ, let us remember, is joy! Let us hope that all of us will have the ineffable experience of it.

—Papal audience, April 19, 1972

**God Is Our Happiness . . . If We Accept It** Our joy is not without tears; but neither do we lack the comfort of a new hope. If the Holy Spirit were to come, would not everything be renewed?

Let us therefore invoke the consoling and vivifying Spirit, addressing ourselves to her who, through the work of the Holy Spirit, gave the world a Savior. —Papal audience, May 21, 1972

**The Pentecost Paradox: The Simultaneity and Succession of Sorrow and Joy** Why these difficulties, these oppositions, these sufferings? Why are these things so? We always ask ourself this question in connection with the fact of Pentecost, which, as we said, dominates the whole life of the Church.

To answer such a question, we would have to be able to penetrate the secrets of divine Providence, that is, the plan of redemption. Let it be enough for us now to suggest a thought for the consolation of those who experience the ineffable fortune of grace and the often no less mysterious fortune of suffering.

What we want to say is simply this, that the two experiences are not only possible together, but compatible. They can be coordinated in a plan of goodness and salvation by the two principles of simultaneity and succession. (One day, we trust, the Lord will reveal to us the wisdom and harmony of this plan.)

The principle of simultaneity means that the Christian can at one same time have two different, opposite experiences, which become complementary: sorrow and joy. He can have two hearts: one natural, the other supernatural. Remember, for example, St. Paul's marvelous expression: "I abound with joy in the midst of all our tribulations" (2 Cor 2:4; 2 Thes 1:4; Acts 5:41). There would be a great deal to say about this complex psychological and spiritual phenomenon.

The other principle, we said, is that of succession. This is the principle which admits that there may be suffering even for the saints — especially for the saints — during this life but which is followed by happiness in the next life. As St. Francis said: "All pain is dear to me, so great is the joy that I await."

In conclusion let us invoke the Holy Spirit as the "Consolator optime," the best consoler!                    —Papal audience, June 26, 1974

**The Challenging Nature of Discipleship**   To live the Christian life well there is need of continual repairing, of recurring reforms, of repeated renewals. The Christian life is not soft or easy. It is not comfortable and a matter of form; it is not blindly optimistic, morally accommodating and spineless. It is joyous but is not happy-go-lucky.          —Papal audience, July 24, 1968

**God Is Joy, but Who Believes Us?**   Let this undaunted certainty remain: God is the true, the supreme happiness of man. Let this stupendous pedagogy remain to teach the catechism to our children, our young pupils; yes, faith is mystery, Christ bears the cross, life is duty, but above all, God is joy....

Now, here is today's question: shall we succeed in making the men of our time understand this religious message; God is joy, our joy? Who listens to us? Who really believes us? (cf. Rom 10:15–16).                    —Papal audience, December 20, 1972

**God Is Our All**   How can the infinite and mysterious greatness of God be the source of our gratitude and at the same time of our joy? Yes, because God is everything for us. God is life, God is power, God is truth, God is goodness, God is beauty; yes, in the end God is our happiness. Alleluia!

How much this surpasses any other inferior conception of religion, which is so often presented under the aspect of distance, darkness, fear, dreadfulness! And how often we have strayed from the study and practice of religion, because we have not realized and joyfully recognized that God is our bliss, our happiness!                    —Papal audience, April 25, 1973

**A Religion of Joy**   We must repeat the angels' announcement of Christmas: "Do not be afraid; behold, I bring you good news of a great joy which will come to all the people" (Lk 2:10).

Yes, our religion is a religion of salvation, a religion of joy. Do we not hear within us, like bells pealing gaily, the echo of the Apostle's exhortations to the Philippians: "Joy to you in the Lord at all times; once again I wish you joy" (4:4)?

This is the true religion, our religion, our spirituality; the joy of God. This is the gift that Christ brings us on being born into the world; the joy of God. —Papal audience, December 20, 1972

**Anticipating the Future with Joy** Let it remain for you, the poor, for you, the afflicted, for you, who hunger for justice and peace, for all of you, who suffer and weep; the kingdom of God is for you, and it is the kingdom of happiness which comforts, compensates, gives truth to hope.

Let it remain for you, who have spiritually chosen Christ: He speaks in your hearts of beatitude and peace. With this ineffable gift He does not, in this life, satisfy your seeking, quench your insatiable thirst; today his happiness is only a sample, an anticipation, a token, an initiation. The fullness of life will come tomorrow, after this earthly day, but it will come, when God's own happiness will be open to those who sought Him and had a foretaste of Him today. God is joy.

—Papal audience, December 20, 1972

**Alleluia** Alleluia is a very ancient traditional acclamation, which comes to us from the Old Testament (cf. Tob 13:22) and which means "praise to God." This acclamation was probably also part of the songs at the ritual supper of the Jews at Passover, and it was therefore uttered by Jesus himself at the end of his last supper (cf. Mt 26:30; Mk 14:26).

It passed into Christian liturgies as an emphatic expression of joy, happiness and strength, reserved especially for Easter time, the time characterized by joy at the celebration of the resurrection of the Lord.

St. Augustine, commenting on the Psalms, reminds us of it, noting that it is not without a secret lesson, because if we must sing Alleluia on certain specific days, we must have it in our heart every day. —Papal audience, April 25, 1973

**A Christian Psychology of Joy**   How often is it repeated and recommended to us; "Be glad in the Lord; I repeat, be glad," says St. Paul to the Philippians (cf. Mt 5:12; 2 Cor 13:11; 1 Th 5:16; 1 Jn 1:4; etc.). A joy that nothing can spoil is a necessary element of the Christian psychology, even in adversities and tribulations: "With all our affliction, I am overjoyed" (2 Cor 7:4).

—Papal audience, July 18, 1973

**Whole-Hearted Christian Efforts Succeed Joyfully**   But let us note, almost in anticipation of the conclusions of our reasoning, that those who aim at complete faithfulness to the Christian vocation in the ways proper to their state, succeed in doing so, and in fact enjoy the effort that this faithfulness requires. They succeed with comparative ease; and this is one of the marvels of Christian life.

Real followers of the Gospel experience it; while those who seek happiness by whittling away faithfulness to Christian life feel its burden, its tedium, and find its demands almost unnatural.          —Papal audience, July 25, 1973

**Grace and Human Effort Make Jesus' Yoke Easy and His Burden Light**   For the Christian to feel fulfilled in his own case by the Lord's words: "My yoke is easy and my burden is light" (Mt 11:30), great courage and loving dedication are necessary.

Then not merely as a result of a psychological law, which teaches us that nothing is difficult for one who loves, but above all because of a marvelous and mysterious process of the helpful intervention of divine grace, we will be able to enjoy an increase of energy, and experience the actual easiness of imitating Christ (cf. Jn 14:18; 2 Cor 12:9; 1 Cor 15:10; etc.).

—Papal audience, July 25, 1973

**Christian Life Is Difficult**   This confident and optimistic view is not belied by another different view of Christian life, which shows us how Christian life is at the same time full of difficulties.

Let us be realistic: Christian life, if we wish to live it genuinely, is difficult. Anyone who tried to deny, or unduly gloss over this difficult aspect, would distort and perhaps even betray the authenticity of Christian life itself. Today this attempt to make it easy, comfortable, effortless, without sacrifice, is in full swing, on the doctrinal and practical planes....

Yes, Christian life is difficult, because it is logical, because it is faithful, because it is strong, because it is militant, because it is great.

May the Lord grant that we understand and live it in this way.

—Papal audience, July 25, 1973

**Preserving Christian Freedom and Joy**   We must do our utmost to preserve for the Christian profession the sense of freedom and joy, which is characteristic of it. We must not weigh it down with burdensome and superfluous laws (cf. Mt 23:4). We must instill in ourselves and in others the taste for things that are true, pure, just, holy, lovely, honest and upright, as St. Paul teaches us (cf. Phil 4:8); and together with the taste, case in incorporating them in our behavior.   —Papal audience, July 25, 1973

Unless otherwise indicated, the following excerpts in this chapter are taken from *Gaudete in Domino* ("On Christian Joy"), May 9, 1975.

**Divine Roots of Joy**   Christian joy could not be properly praised if one were to remain indifferent to the outward and inward witness that God the Creator renders to Himself in the midst of His creation: "And God saw that it was good" (Gen 1:10, 12, 18, 21, 25, 31). Raising up man in the setting of a universe that is the work of His power, wisdom and love, and even before manifesting Himself personally according to the mode of revelation, God disposes the mind and heart of His creature to meet joy, at the same time as truth.

**The Quest for Happiness and Fulfillment**   When he awakens to the world, does not man feel, in addition to the natural desire to understand and take possession of it, the desire to find within it his fulfillment and happiness?...

As everyone knows, there are several degrees of this "happiness." Its most noble expression is joy, or "happiness" in the strict sense, when man, on the level of his higher faculties, finds his peace and satisfaction in the possession of a known and loved good.

**Joy Is Born of Harmony**    Man experiences joy when he finds himself in harmony with nature, and especially in the encounter, sharing and communion with other people.

**Mystics in Our Midst**    Poets, artists, thinkers, but also ordinary men and women, simply disposed to a certain inner light, have been able and still are able, in the times before Christ and in our own time and among us, to experience something of the joy of God.

**The Transitory Nature of Joy**    But how can we ignore the additional fact that joy is always imperfect, fragile and threatened? By a strange paradox, the consciousness of that which, beyond all passing pleasure, would constitute true happiness, also includes the certainty that there is no perfect happiness. The experience of finiteness, felt by each generation in its turn, obliges one to acknowledge and to plumb the immense gap that always exists between reality and the desire for the infinite. This paradox, and this difficulty in attaining joy, seem to us particularly acute today.

**Distinguishing Joy from Pleasure**    Technological society has succeeded in multiplying the opportunities for pleasure, but it has great difficulty in generating joy. For joy comes from another source. It is spiritual.

In many regions and sometimes in our midst, the sum of physical and moral sufferings weighs heavily: so many starving people, so many victims of fruitless combats, so many people torn from their homes!

These miseries are perhaps not deeper than those of the past but they have taken on a worldwide dimension. They are better known, reported by the mass media — at least as much as the events of good fortune — and they overwhelm people's minds.

Often there seems to be no adequate human solution to them. This situation nevertheless cannot hinder us from speaking about joy and hoping for joy. It is indeed in the midst of their distress that our fellow men need to know joy, to hear its song.

Yes, because Christ was "a man like us in all things but sin" (Heb 4:15). He accepted and experienced affective and spiritual joys, as a gift of God. And He did not rest until "to the poor he proclaimed the good news of salvation... and to those in sorrow, joy" (Lk 4:18). The Gospel of St. Luke particularly gives witness to this seed of joy.

**Joy's Minimum Standard of Living**   People must obviously unite their efforts to secure at least a minimum of relief, well-being, security and justice, necessary for happiness, for the many peoples deprived of them. Such solidarity is already the work of God, it corresponds to Christ's commandment. Already it secures peace, restores hope, strength, communion, and gives access to joy, for the one who gives as for the one who receives, for it is more blessed to give than to receive (cf. Acts 20:35)....

For joy cannot be dissociated from sharing. In God Himself, all is joy because all is giving.

**Daily Opportunities for Joy**   There is also needed a patient effort to teach people, or teach them once more, how to savor in a simple way the many human joys that the Creator places in our path:

the elating joy of existence and of life;

the joy of chaste and sanctified love;

the peaceful joy of nature and silence;

the sometimes austere joy of work well done;

the joy and satisfaction of duty performed;

the transparent joy of purity, service and sharing;

the demanding joy of sacrifice.

The Christian will be able to purify, complete and sublimate these joys; he will not be able to disdain them.

**Repentance Leads to Joy**    Who does not recall the words of
St. Augustine: "You have made us for Yourself, Lord, and our
hearts are restless until they rest in You"? It is therefore by
becoming more present to God, by turning away from sin, that
man can truly enter into spiritual joy.

Without doubt "flesh and blood" (cf. Mt 16:17) are incapable
of this. But Revelation can open up this possibility and grace
can bring about this return.

**Jesus' Joys**    The depth of His interior life did not blunt His
concrete attitude or His sensitivity.

He admires the birds of heaven, the lilies of the field.

He immediately grasps God's attitude toward creation at the
dawn of history.

He willingly extols the joy of the sower and the harvester,
the joy of the man who finds a hidden treasure, the joy of the
shepherd who recovers his sheep or of the woman who finds
her lost coin, the joy of those invited to the feast, the joy of
a marriage celebration, the joy of the father who embraces his
son returning from a prodigal life, and the joy of the woman who
has just brought her child into the world.

For Jesus, these joys are real because for Him they are the
signs of the spiritual joys of the kingdom of God: the joy of
people who enter this kingdom return there or work there, the
joy of the Father who welcomes them.

And for His part Jesus Himself manifests His satisfaction and
His tenderness when He meets children wishing to approach
Him, a rich young man who is faithful and wants to do more,
friends who open their home to Him, like Martha, Mary and
Lazarus.

His happiness is above all to see the Word accepted, the possessed delivered, a sinful woman or a publican like Zacchaeus
converted, a widow taking from her poverty and giving. He even
exults with joy when He states that the little ones have the revelation of the kingdom which remains hidden from the wise and
able (cf. Lk 10:21).

**The Secret of Jesus' Joy**   But it is necessary here below to understand properly the secret of the unfathomable joy which dwells in Jesus and which is special to Him. It is especially the Gospel of St. John that lifts the veil, by giving us the intimate words of the Son of God made man. If Jesus radiates such peace, such assurance, such happiness, such availability, it is by reason of the inexpressible love by which He knows that He is loved by His Father.

**Sharing in Jesus' Joy**   And the disciples and all those who believe in Christ are called to share this joy. Jesus wishes them to have in themselves His joy in its fullness (cf. Jn 17:13). "I have made your name known to them and will continue to make it known, so that the love with which you loved me may be in them, and so that I may be in them" (Jn 17:26).

**Christian Joy Begins on Earth**   This joy of living in God's love begins here below. It is the joy of the kingdom of God. But it is granted on a steep road which requires a total confidence in the Father and in the Son, and a preference given to the kingdom.

**A Demanding Joy Proclaimed by the Beatitudes**   The message of Jesus promises above all joy — this demanding joy; and does it not begin with the beatitudes?

**Sharing in Divine and Human Joy**   In essence, Christian joy is the spiritual sharing in the unfathomable joy, both divine and human, which is in the heart of Jesus Christ glorified. As soon as God the Father begins to manifest in history the mystery of His will, according to His purpose which He set forth in Christ as a plan for the fullness of time (cf. Eph 1:9–10), this joy is mysteriously announced in the midst of the People of God, before its identity has been unveiled.

**The Mysterious Paradox of Paschal Joy**   It remains that, here below, the joy of the kingdom brought to realization can only spring from the simultaneous celebration of the death and resurrection of the Lord.

This is the paradox of the Christian condition which sheds particular light on that of the human condition: neither trials nor sufferings have been eliminated from this world, but they take on a new meaning in the certainty of sharing in the redemption wrought by the Lord and of sharing in His glory.

This is why the Christian, though subject to the difficulties of human life, is not reduced to groping for the way; nor does he see in death the end of his hopes....

The Easter Exultet sings of a mystery accomplished beyond the hopes of the prophets: in the joyful announcement of the resurrection, even man's suffering finds itself transformed, while the fullness of joy springs from the victory of the Crucified, from His pierced heart and His glorified body....

This life, being animated by a zealous love of the Lord and His brethren, is necessarily exercised under the standard of the paschal sacrifice, going through love to death, and through death to life and love....

Paschal joy is not just that of a possible transfiguration: it is the joy of the new presence of the Risen Christ dispensing to His own the Holy Spirit, so that He may dwell with them....

This positive outlook on people and things, the fruit of an enlightened human spirit and the fruit of the Holy Spirit, finds in Christians a privileged place of replenishment: the celebration of the Paschal Mystery of Jesus. In His passion, death and resurrection, Christ summarizes the history of each man and of all men, with their weight of sufferings and sins, with their capacities for progress and holiness.

**Paschal Joy: The Style of Christian Spirituality**  Paschal joy is the style of Christian spirituality; it is not superficial thoughtlessness; it is wisdom nourished by the three theological virtues. It is not exterior and noisy merriment: it is joy that springs from deep inward motives. Nor, far less, is it hedonistic surrender to the easy pleasures of instinctive and uncontrolled passions, but it is strength of spirit that knows, wills, loves; it is the exultation of new life that invades simultaneously the word and the soul.

—Papal audience, April 19, 1972

**Transfigured Joy**   The humble human joys in our lives, which are like seeds of a higher reality are transfigured. Here below this joy will always include to a certain extent the painful trial of a woman in travail and a certain apparent abandonment, like that of the orphan: tears and lamentation, while the world parades its gloating satisfaction. But the disciples' sadness, which is according to God and not according to the world, will be promptly changed into a spiritual joy that no one will be able to take away from them (cf. Jn 16:20–22; 2 Cor 1:4, 7:46). Such is the situation of Christian existence, and very particularly of the apostolic life.

**Many Paths to Joy**   Nevertheless, there are many dwellings in the Father's house, and for those whose heart is consumed by the Holy Spirit many ways of dying to themselves and of coming to the holy joy of the resurrection. The shedding of blood is not the only path.

**The Passion of Love**   Yet the combat for the kingdom necessarily includes passing through a passion of love, which the spiritual masters have spoken of in excellent ways. And here their interior experiences meet, in the very diversity of mystical traditions, in the East as in the West. They attest to the same path for the soul: per crucem ad lucem, and from this world to the Father, in the life — giving breath of the Spirit. Each of these spiritual masters has left us a message of joy.

**St. Francis of Assisi**   We would like to evoke more especially three figures that are still very attractive today for the Christian people as a whole. First of all, the poor man of Assisi, in whose footsteps numbers of Holy Year pilgrims are endeavoring to follow. Having left everything for the Lord, St. Francis rediscovers through holy poverty something, so to speak, of the original blessedness, when the world came forth intact from the hands of the Creator.

In the most extreme abnegation, half blind, he was able to chant the unforgettable Canticle of the Creatures, the praise of our brother the sun, of all nature, which had become transparent for him and like a pure mirror of God's glory. He could even express joy at the arrival of "our sister bodily death": "Blessed are those who will be conformed to your most Holy will. . . . "

**St. Thérèse of Lisieux**    In more recent times, St. Thérèse of Lisieux shows us the courageous way of abandonment into the hands of God to whom she entrusts her littleness.

And yet it is not that she has no experience of the feeling of God's absence, a feeling which our century is harshly experiencing; "Sometimes it seems that the little bird (to which she compared herself) cannot believe that anything else exists except the clouds that envelop it. . . . This is the moment of perfect joy for the poor, weak little thing. . . . What happiness for it to remain there nevertheless, and to gaze at the invisible light that hides from its faith."

**St. Maximilian Kolbe**    And then how could one fail to recall the luminous figure and example for our generation of Blessed [now Saint] Maximilian Kolbe, the authentic disciple of St. Francis? In the most tragic trials which have bloodied our age, he offered himself voluntarily to death in order to save an unknown brother, and the witnesses report that his interior peace, serenity and joy somehow transformed the place of suffering — which was usually like an image of hell — into the antechamber of eternal life, both for his unfortunate companions and for himself.

**Joy and Communion**    Joy is the result of a human-divine communion, and aspires to a communion ever more universal. In no way can it encourage the person who enjoys it to have an attitude of preoccupation with self.

Joy gives the heart a catholic openness to the world of people, at the same time that it wounds the heart with a longing for eternal bliss. Among the fervent, joy deepens their awareness of being exiles, but it guards them from the temptation to desert the place of their combat for the coming of the kingdom.

**Rediscovering Daily Joys**   We include also all those who are deeply involved in family, professional and social responsibility. The burden of their charges, in a fast-moving world, too often prevents them from enjoying daily joys. Nevertheless such joys do exist. The Holy Spirit wants to help these people rediscover these joys, to purify them, to share them.

**Suffering Transfigured into Joy**   We think of the world of the suffering, we think of all those who have reached the evening of their lives. God's joy is knocking at the door of their physical and moral sufferings, not indeed with irony, but to achieve therein His paradoxical work of transfiguration.

**Fidelity to Conscience and the Road to Joy**   Our heart and mind turn also to all those who live beyond the visible sphere of the People of God. By bringing their lives into harmony with the innermost appeal of their conscience, which is the echo of God's voice, they are on the road to joy.

**Conversion Is a Step Forward**   The Lord wishes above all to make us understand that the conversion demanded of us is in no way a backward step, as sin is. It is rather a setting out, an advancement in true freedom and in joy. It is the response to an invitation coming from Him — an invitation that is loving, respectful and pressing at the same time: "Come to me, all you who labor and are overburdened, and I will give you rest. Shoulder my yoke and learn from me, for I am gentle and humble in heart, and you will find rest for your souls!" (Mt 11:28–29).

**Joy Fills the Heart**   The joy of being Christian, of being united with the Church, of being "in Christ," and in the state of grace with God, is truly able to fill the human heart. Is it not this profound exultation that gives an overwhelming accent to the Memorial of Pascal: "Joy, joy, joy, tears of joy"?

**Literary Heralds of Joy**   And near to us, how many writers there are who know how to express in a new form — we are thinking, for example, of Georges Bernanos — this evangelical

joy of the humble which shines forth everywhere in the world
and which speaks of God's silence! Joy always springs from a
certain outlook on man and on God. "When your eye is sound,
your whole body too is filled with light" (Lk 11:34).

**Christian Communities Should Be Centers of Optimism Rather
Than Criticism**    Let the agitated members of various groups
therefore reject the excesses of systematic and destructive
criticism!

Without departing from a realistic viewpoint, let Christian
communities become centers of optimism where all the members resolutely endeavor to perceive the positive aspect of
people and events.

"Love does not rejoice in what is wrong but rejoices with the
truth. There is no limit to love's forbearance, to its trust, its
hope, its power to endure" (1 Cor 13:6–7). The attainment of
such an outlook is not just a matter of psychology. It is also a
fruit of the Holy Spirit.

**The Spirit Underlying Joy**    This Spirit, who dwells fully in the
person of Jesus, made Him during His earthly life so alert to the
joys of daily life, so tactful and persuasive for putting sinners
back on the road to a new youth of heart and mind!

It is this same Spirit who animated the Blessed Virgin and
each of the saints.

It is this same Spirit who still today gives to so many Christians the joy of living day by day their particular vocation, in
the peace and hope which surpass setbacks and sufferings.

It is the Spirit of Pentecost who today leads very many followers of Christ along the paths of prayer, in the cheerfulness
of filial praise, toward the humble and joyous service of the
disinherited and of those on the margins of society....

The Holy Spirit is given to the Church as the inexhaustible
principle of her joy as the bride of the glorified Christ. He
recalls to her mind, through the ministry of grace and truth
exercised by the successors of the apostles, the very teaching
of the Lord.

# Conclusion

Joy should accompany our *lectio divina* of Paul's teaching and modeling of Christian joy. Not the superficial joy of temporary exhilaration, but a deeper, abiding joy rooted in enduring Christian values. Because it involves the whole person in a series of interrelated steps responsive to the Spirit, the source of Christian joy, *lectio* enables us to tap into this.

*Lectio* and Paul in combination elicit joy because they are dialogically based. Communications remind us that we are not alone and enable us to identify and share with others. The first human joy in the Bible is Adam's upon encountering Eve and breaking what John Paul II refers to as the circle of solitude. Henceforth communication and identity development and corresponding fulfillment is possible through human interaction. An attested and accessible path to Christian joy is *lectio* of God's word and orthodox teaching on the subject such as Paul's.

Cardinal Martini once commented that Paul was "a man who knew how to praise.... He was a man who, precisely because he was deeply conscious of the suffering and tragedies of human life, knew how to rise to a very high quality of praise." Suffering often precedes joy. *Lectio* helps us to drink in Paul's wisdom and enthusiasm and manifest it in our life through prayer and application. Joy's hopeful ends and divine source give us reason to join Paul and his New Testament namesake in rejoicing in the Lord (cf. Phil 4:4).

## Chapter 14

# Evangelization

*Whatever may be the opinion you have of the Pontiff of Rome, you know our mission. We are the bearer of a message for all mankind. And this we are, not only in our own personal name; but also in that of those Christian brethren who share the same sentiments which we express here, particularly of those who so kindly charged us explicitly to be their spokesperson here.*

*Like a messenger who, after a long journey, finally succeeds in delivering the letter which has been entrusted to him, so we appreciate the good fortune of this moment, however brief, which fulfills a desire nourished in the heart for nearly twenty centuries.*

*For, as you will remember, we are very ancient; we here represent a long history; we here celebrate the epilogue of a wearying pilgrimage in search of a conversation with the entire world, ever since the command was given to us: Go and bring the good news to all peoples. Now, you here represent all peoples. Allow us to tell you that we have a message, a happy message, to deliver to each one of you and to all.*

— Pope Paul VI, Address to the
U.N. General Assembly, October 4, 1965

It would be difficult to identify in the entire history of the Church as long a period of time in which it was led by outstanding pontiffs. John XXIII, Paul VI, and John Paul II will surely go down as among the greatest popes of all time, and Pius XII will be recognized as the pope who made possible Vatican II and the Church's *aggiornamento* (the Italian word meaning "updating," which John XXIII used with respect to his renewal initiatives) possible through his insightful and mostly progressive encyclicals.

One of the characteristics of these popes, and indeed most great spiritual persons, is their sense of timing, human needs, and the symbolic dimensions of human actions.

In 1974 the Church held a synod on evangelization. It spawned dialogue and good ideas, but in a variety of directions and without any comprehensible synthesis. This is where Paul VI came in.

On the feast of the Immaculate Conception, December 8, 1975, Paul issued his final pastoral letter, the apostolic exhortation *Evangelii Nuntiandi* ("On Evangelization in the Modern World"). It was a fitting climax to his publications in the sense that it revealed that he had come full circle and matured in his response to the evolving world.

Paul's first encyclical, *Ecclesiam Suam* ("Paths of the Church"), identified dialogue — reciprocal, open communications deepened by spiritual and moral values — as a fundamental path of the Church in the modern world amid the changes and clarifications sought by Vatican II. Building on the initiatives and spirit of his predecessor, John XXIII, he urged the Church to continue its renewal of self-understanding and both internal and external relations. Attitudes, values, and actions undertaken and refined in light of the Gospel were the appropriate response to the signs of the times that Paul and the council fathers were discerning.

A decade later, much had changed and a renewed and refined response was called for. Understanding the context and purpose of this apostolic exhortation sheds much light on the state of the Church and the world at the end of Paul's pontificate, and the path the Church had taken under Paul's leadership. It is also a fitting way to close our reflections on the life, papacy, and teachings of Paul VI.

## Paul's Long and Winding Road

When Paul VI assumed the papacy in the midst of Vatican II, there was reason for both concern and optimism. Concern because the Armageddon-threatening Cuban Missile Crisis occurred less than a year earlier and the Cold War was at its peak. Civil wars in Asia and Africa were accompanied by mass starvation and poverty levels incongruous with the technological and material advances and resources of first world countries.

Within the Church, the expected struggle over the ideological direction of the council had ensued, causing several documents, particularly the Dogmatic Constitutions on the Church and Divine Revelation to undergo tumultuous debate and revision, much of it behind the scenes and involving some of the most powerful persons in the Church.

As a diplomat and former secretary of state, Paul VI was well equipped to help the Church navigate theological, ecumenical, and internal minefields. He wasn't going to win any popularity contests, but at least the Church would stay united and have a comprehensible direction to follow. Traversing this path would prove difficult given the diverse compasses used (i.e., the contrasting agendas of traditionalists and progressives) and the unfamiliar ground that the Church was traveling.

What Paul VI and the council fathers were to discover was that the world was increasingly embracing the path of secularism and had little interest in entering into serious dialogue and cooperation with the Church. Further, Paul and the fathers underestimated the confusion, distortions, resistance, and conflicts that would mar the communication and implementation of council teachings and reforms.

When it became apparent that the disposition to dialogue would be insufficient as a communications agenda, the Church turned to its missionary roots and renewed its evangelization efforts. The increasingly secular mentality not only of the world but also of many in the Church indicated that a conversion process was needed and that, as Paul wrote in his apostolic exhortation, the first persons who must undergo evangelization are members of the Church. The evangelizer begins by being evangelized. Before we can authentically and convincingly share the good news with others, we must assimilate and exemplify it ourselves.

Through most of his pontificate (with the exception of the birth control question, where Paul underestimated the resistance he would experience within the Church and particularly at the clerical and episcopal level), Paul had his finger on the pulse of modern culture and mentalities, both sacred and secular. In his first encyclical he imparted communication and spirituality principles necessary for authentic dialogue. In his final letter, Paul built on these to illustrate how to spread the good news about Jesus.

Paul was apt at communicating his message, even though many failed to listen — thereby reminding us of what to expect — because his pontificate had been for him a continual call to conversion and trust in the Lord: "Perhaps the Lord has called me to this service not because I have any aptitude for it, nor so that I can govern the Church in its present difficulties, but so that I may suffer something and thus that it may be clear that it is the Lord, and no one else, who guides and saves it. In the pope's life there are no times of rest or respite. Fatherhood is never suspended. And since what he is dealing with always goes beyond the bounds of possibility, the only solution he has is to abandon himself to the present moment, which is the Lord. A pope lives from crisis to crisis, from moment to moment. He goes, like the Hebrews in the desert, from manna to manna. And he has not much time to look back on the road he has traveled or forward to the way that lies ahead."

The common theme in Paul's first and last pastoral letter was communications. How do we reach out to others, share the good news, and cooperate with God in building up the kingdom? What social and communication principles and practices must be integrated with moral and spiritual principles in order to impart, receive, and implement the message effectively? Paul's diplomatic experience had provided him with excellent insights into this process, which combined with his deep spirituality and cultural sensitivities enabled him to impart a comprehensible and apt message.

An attribute of Paul VI that was frequently mentioned by those who knew him was his understanding of and empathy for modern persons. He understood the mentality and concerns of his audience. Unlike John Paul II, who often appeared in great conflict with contemporary society, Paul was able to relate to it in an observant and nonintimidating manner without compromising Christian values or objectives.

For example, Paul gathered artists to the Sistine Chapel in 1964 and addressed the role of art in the Church and Christian spirituality.

He assigned his personal secretary, Pasquale Macchi, to oversee the development of a modern art section of the Vatican Museum. This opened in 1973 to excellent reviews.

Responding to the pope's appeal and initiative, modern art from all over the world flowed in to the Vatican, far more than they could ever display. Paul's contributions were subsequently recognized in a number of tributes, including a 1999 exhibit entitled *Paul VI, A Light for Art* hosted by the Cathedral Museum of Milan and the Charlemagne Wing of the Vatican Museums.

Paul had his own art collection and record player. His aesthetic appreciation helped him understand the culture and formulate a message comprehensible to modern persons.

In order to evangelize the world effectively, you must connect with it. Missionaries recognize the importance of communicating the Gospel message in ways suited to the audience's mentality and culture. Particularly during his trips to Africa, where the Church was experiencing considerable growth, John Paul II frequently addressed the degree and ways in which Christianity, particularly liturgical and devotional practices, could be absorbed into the existing culture without compromising either.

Paul recognized that when communications are impaired and the dialogue does not occur in an optimal way, the message of the Gospel must still be sent forth — even when it appears doomed to rejection, as was the case with many of Paul's initiatives and teachings. Because Paul continually exercised his evangelical mission, sharing the good news amid trials, hardships, and opposition, he was able to distill the insights of the 1974 Synod into a comprehensible message of hope for the world.

Paul reminds us that while evangelization is not a process of imposing Christianity on others, neither is it something that occurs of itself. Each of us must contribute, beginning with hearing and heeding the message. Conversion is as central a theme in Paul's letter as evangelization. The two go together. Throughout his papacy Paul used the symbols and language of the day along with his own personal gestures to present the Christian message in a comprehensible, compelling, and authentic manner.

Like Jesus in the Gospels, Paul advocated spiritual renewal, in biblical parlance, repentance, and conversion. Both evangelizers began by communicating with the people in simple ways compatible with their audience's background and lot in life. Jesus used familiar farming, pastoral, and nature images in his parables, and healed people through their faith in both verbal and physical encounters.

The people's circumstances and faith, or lack thereof, rather than abstract concepts or stringent moral principles was the starting point for the evangelical and therapeutic encounter. Before they would be able to live the message, they had to discover the efficacy and personal meaning of their faith. Both Paul and Jesus engaged their audience in dialogue in order to help them discover their real needs and wounds and what was necessary to grow and heal.

Jesus' healings and teachings always had an evangelical dimension. Conversion and not just physical and psychological health was necessary for wholeness. His parting message in Matthew's Gospel, the Great Commission (cf. Mt 28:20), brings these elements together.

Like all good missionaries, Jesus and Paul were willing to assume the risks that evangelization entails, chiefly rejection and persecution. Am I?

## Paul's Evangelical Consummation

Paul's literary contributions during his pontificate ended in the same way as the Gospels: we must teach, preach, and heal, and spread the message wherever we can. Even when the dialogue is impeded by human weakness, the Spirit continues its work (cf. Rom 8). By ending on an evangelical note, Paul brought the Church back to the Christian communications theme with which he had begun his pontificate.

Paul's life and mission were about to end. However, the message and charisms entrusted to him live on in the Spirit through our receptivity to ongoing conversion and evangelical dispositions, communications, and actions.

Paul's first apostolic exhortation, in 1975, highlighted the joy that accompanies the Christian vocation. His second and final one gave it expression and a charter based on the message of the Gospels that Paul would literally take to his grave: "Paul, who had such a wonderful sense of the meaningful gesture, planned his funeral with an eye to making it sum up his life. His coffin was on ground level. It was surmounted not by the tiara that he had given away, not even by a miter or a stole, but by the open book of the Gospels, its pages riffled by the light breeze" (Yves Congar).

Let us conclude our introduction to this final chapter the way we did the first chapter, with Cardinal Martini's inspiring and instructive recollections: "It can be said that Paul VI repeated the process of presenting the 'different' within the 'commonplace.' Like few persons of our time he succeeded in awakening in today's people the thrill of mystery. He stirred up amazement for the exceptional, unique, absolute figure of Christ and the sense of the superhuman realities contained in the totally human life of the Church. But he did all this using the potentiality, the nuances and the resources — together with the limits, the opaqueness and the subtlety of the language, the sensitivity, the mentality and the culture of today.

"He was a believer and a master of the faith who spoke not just 'to' today's people but 'as' one of them. His faith was so limpid and mature that he was able to express himself even in the era and the culture of disbelief, of secularization, of a grown-up humanity proud of its progress but desperate because of its loneliness. And his assimilation of contemporary culture was so interior, so personalized, so critically sensitive that he was able to discern in it the backward glances, the contradictions, and the secret chinks through which it could prepare to accept the message of faith....

"Now he is alive in the Resurrection of Jesus, in Whose glorious Transfiguration sign he closed his eyes on earthly cares. He is interceding for all his friends, for the whole Church he tenderly loved and also for the peoples of those lands visited by Jesus for whom he did so much and suffered so much. We, too, on this day, remember him as one of the 'great friends' who let us feel on earth the joy born of the Risen Lord.'"*

Through our encounters with Paul and the befriending that ensues we can relate to Cardinal Martini's testimony.

---

*Cardinal Carlo Maria Martini, *Journeying with the Lord* (Staten Island, N.Y.: Alba House, 1987), 278; reprinted with permission.

# EVANGELIZATION

Unless otherwise indicated, all quotations in this chapter are from the apostolic exhortation *Evangelii Nuntiandi* ("On Evangelization in the Modern World"), December 8, 1975.

**The Validity of Other Faiths**   Recognizing also the existence, outside the organism of the Church of Christ, of numerous elements of truth and sanctification which belong to her as her own and tend to Catholic unity, and believing in the action of the Holy Spirit who stirs up in the heart of the disciples of Christ love of this unity, we entertain the hope that the Christians who are not yet in the full communion of the one only Church will one day be reunited in one flock with one only shepherd.

We believe that the Church is necessary for salvation, because Christ, who is the sole mediator and way of salvation, renders Himself present for us in His body which is the Church.

But the divine design of salvation embraces all men; and those who without fault on their part do not know the Gospel of Christ and His Church, but seek God sincerely, and under the influence of grace endeavor to do His will as recognized through the promptings of their conscience, they, in a number known only to God, can obtain salvation.

— "Credo" of the People of God, July 30, 1968

**The Christian Antidote to Modern Pessimism**   And we are to preach the Gospel in this extraordinary period of human history, a time surely without precedent, in which peaks of achievement never before attained are matched by similarly unprecedented depths of bewilderment and despair.

If ever there were a time when Christians were challenged to be, more than ever before, a light to illumine the world, a city on a hill, a salt to give savour to men's lives (cf. Mt 5:13–14), surely that time is now! For we possess the antidote to the pessimism, the gloomy foreboding, the dejection and fear, which afflict our time.

We have good news! And every one of us, by the very nature of his Christianity, must feel himself impelled to broadcast this good news to the ends of the earth. "We cannot but speak of what we have seen and heard" (Acts 4:20)....

We must tell men, and keep on telling them, that "the key, the focal point, and the goal of human history" is to be found in our Lord and Master.

We must tell that this is true not only for believers, but also applies to everyone, for whom Christ died and whose ultimate vocation is to correspond to God's design: "to unite all things in him, things in heaven and things on earth" (Eph 1:10).

—Mission Sunday, June 25, 1971

**The Good News: We Are Not Alone**   The good news is this: that God loves us; that he became man to share in our life and to share his life with us; that he walks with us — every step of the way — taking our concerns as his own, for he cares about us (1 Pt 5:7); and that therefore men are not alone, for God is present in their entire history, that of peoples and that of individuals; that he will bring us, if we allow him, to an eternal happiness beyond the bounds of human expectation.

—Mission Sunday, June 25, 1971

**Christ's Humble Model of Evangelization**   Did not Christ himself frequently beg from those near him the means by which he chose to accomplish good?

Did he not feed the multitude with a few loaves given by a boy in the crowd?

Did he not beg the use of a fisherman's boat from which he might speak the word of life to the people?

Did he not readily accept the assistance offered to him and his disciples by the women who provided for them out of their own resources?

Did he not ride on a borrowed ass down to the place of his Passion?

And was he not dependent on a rich man for the very tomb from which he accomplished his Resurrection?

—Mission Sunday, June 25, 1971

**The Centrality of the Kingdom of God**   As an evangelizer, Christ first of all proclaims a kingdom, the kingdom of God; and this is so important that by comparison, everything else becomes "the rest," which is "given in addition." Only the kingdom therefore is absolute, and it makes everything else relative. The Lord will delight in describing in many ways the happiness of belonging to this kingdom (a paradoxical happiness which is made up of things that the world rejects), the demands of the kingdom and its Magna Charta, the heralds of the kingdom, its mysteries, its children, the vigilance and fidelity demanded of whoever awaits its definitive coming. . . .

All of this is begun during the life of Christ and definitively accomplished by His death and resurrection. But it must be patiently carried on during the course of history, in order to be realized fully on the day of the final coming of Christ, whose date is known to no one except the Father.

**Blood, Sweat, and Tears Are Necessary for Salvation**   This kingdom and this salvation, which are the key words of Jesus Christ's evangelization, are available to every human being as grace and mercy and yet at the same time each individual must gain them by force — they belong to the violent, says the Lord, through toil and suffering, through a life lived according to the Gospel, through abnegation and the cross, through the spirit of the beatitudes. But above all each individual gains them through a total interior renewal which the Gospel calls metanoia; it is a radical conversion, a profound change of mind and heart.

**The Preaching of the Word**   Christ accomplished this proclamation of the kingdom of God through the untiring preaching of a word which, it will be said, has no equal elsewhere: "Here is a teaching that is new, and with authority behind it. 'And he won the approval of all, and they were astonished by the gracious words that came from his lips.' There has never been anybody who has spoken like him." His words reveal the secret of God, His plan and His promise, and there by change the heart of man and his destiny.

**Evangelization Begins with Being Evangelized**   The Church is an evangelizer, but she begins by being evangelized herself. She is the community of believers, the community of hope lived and communicated, the community of brotherly love; and she needs to listen unceasingly to what she must believe, to her reasons for hoping, to the new commandment of love. She is the People of God immersed in the world, and often tempted by idols, and she always needs to hear the proclamation of the "mighty works of God" which converted her to the Lord; she always needs to be called together afresh by Him and reunited. In brief, this means that she has a constant need of being evangelized, if she wishes to retain freshness, vigor and strength in order to proclaim the Gospel.

**Evangelism Implies Conversion**   For the Church, evangelizing means bringing the good news into all the strata of humanity, and through its influence transforming humanity from within and making it new: "Now I am making the whole of creation new." But there is now new humanity if there are not first of all new persons renewed by baptism and by lives lived according to the Gospel. The purpose of evangelization is therefore precisely this interior change, and if it had to be expressed in one sentence the best way of stating it would be to say that the Church evangelizes when she seeks to convert, solely through the divine power of the message she proclaims, both the personal and collective consciences of people, the activities in which they engage, and the lives and concrete milieu which are theirs.

**The Transforming Tentacles of the Gospel**   Strata of humanity which are transformed: for the Church it is a question not only of preaching the Gospel in ever wider geographic areas or to ever greater numbers of people, but also of affecting and as it were upsetting, through the power of the Gospel, mankind's criteria of judgement, determining values, points of interest, lines of thought, sources of inspiration and models of life, which are in contrast with the Word of God and the plan of salvation.

**Evangelizing Cultures**   What matters is to evangelize man's culture and cultures (not in a purely decorative way, as it were, by applying a thin veneer, but in a vital way, in depth and right to their very roots), in the wide and rich sense which these terms have in *Gaudium et Spes,* always taking the person as one's starting-point and always coming back to the relationships of people among themselves and with God....

Though independent of cultures, the Gospel and evangelization are not necessarily incompatible with them; rather they are capable of permeating them all without becoming subject to any one of them.

The split between the Gospel and culture is without a doubt the drama of our time just as it was of other times. Therefore every effort must be made to ensure a full evangelization of culture, or more correctly of cultures. They have to be regenerated by an encounter with the Gospel. But this encounter will not take place if the Gospel is not proclaimed.

**Share the Word**   Finally, the person who has been evangelized goes on to evangelize others. Here lies the test of truth, the touchstone of evangelization: it is unthinkable that a person should accept the Word and give himself to the kingdom without becoming a person who bears witness to it and proclaims it in his turn.

**The Spiritual Charter of Evangelism**   Evangelization therefore also includes the preaching of hope in the promises made by God in the new Covenant in Jesus Christ; the preaching of God's love for us and of our love for God; the preaching of brotherly love for all men — the capacity of giving and forgiving, of self-denial, of helping one's brother and sister — which, springing from the love of God, is the kernel of the Gospel; the preaching of the mystery of evil and of the active search for good. The preaching likewise — and this is always urgent — of the search for God Himself through prayer which is principally that of adoration and thanksgiving, but also through communion with the visible sign of the encounter with God which is the Church of Jesus Christ; and this communion in its turn is expressed by the application of those other signs of Christ living and acting in the Church which are the sacraments.

**Lasting Liberation Is Rooted in God and Conversion**   And what is more, the Church has the firm conviction that all temporal liberation, all political liberation — even if it endeavors to find its justification in such or such a page of the Old or New Testament, even if it claims for its ideological postulates and its norms of action theological data and conclusions, even if it pretends to be today's theology — carries within itself the germ of its own negation and fails to reach the ideal that it proposes for itself whenever its profound motives are not those of justice in charity, whenever its zeal lacks a truly spiritual dimension and whenever its final goal is not salvation and happiness in God.

The Church considers it to be undoubtedly important to build up structures which are more human, more just, more respectful of the rights of the person and less oppressive and less enslaving, but she is conscious that the best structures and the most idealized systems soon become inhuman if the inhuman inclinations of the human heart are not made wholesome, if those who live in these structures or who rule them do not undergo a conversion of heart and of outlook.

**Example Is the First Means of Evangelization**   For the Church, the first means of evangelization is the witness of an authentically Christian life, given over to God in a communion that nothing should destroy and at the same time given to one's neighbor with limitless zeal. As we said recently to a group of lay people, "modern man listens more willingly to witnesses than to teachers, and if he does listen to teachers, it is because they are witnesses."

**Collective Evangelization**   Our century is characterized by the mass media or means of social communication, and the first proclamation, catechesis or the further deepening of faith cannot do without these means, as we have already emphasized. When they are put at the service of the Gospel, they are capable of increasing almost indefinitely the area in which the Word of God is heard; they enable the good news to reach millions of people. The Church would feel guilty before the Lord if she did not utilize these powerful means that human skill is daily rendering more perfect.

**One-on-One Evangelization**   For this reason, side by side with the collective proclamation of the Gospel, the other form of transmission, the person-to-person one, remains valid and important. The Lord often used it (for example, with Nicodemus, Zacchaeus, the Samaritan woman, Simon the Pharisee), and so did the apostles. In the long run, is there any other way of handing on the Gospel than by transmitting to another person one's personal experience of faith?

**Evangelization and the Sacraments**   In a certain sense it is a mistake to make a contrast between evangelization and sacramentalization, as is sometimes done. It is indeed true that a certain way of administering the sacraments, without the solid support of catechesis regarding these same sacraments and a global catechesis, could end up by depriving them of their effectiveness to a great extent. The role of evangelization is precisely to educate people in the faith in such a way as to lead each individual Christian to live the sacraments as true sacraments of faith — and not to receive them passively or reluctantly.

**Distinguishing Secularism and Secularization**   From the spiritual point of view, the modern world seems to be forever immersed in what a modern author has termed "the drama of atheistic humanism." On the one hand one is forced to note in the very heart of this contemporary world the phenomenon which is becoming almost its most striking characteristic: secularism. We are not speaking of secularization, which is the effort, in itself just and legitimate and in no way incompatible with faith or religion, to discover in creation, in each thing or each happening in the universe, the laws which regulate them with a certain autonomy, but with the inner conviction that the Creator has placed these laws there. The last council has in this sense affirmed the legitimate autonomy of culture and particularly of the sciences. Here we are thinking of a true secularism: a concept to the world according to which the latter is self-explanatory, without any need for recourse to God, who thus becomes superfluous and an encumbrance. This sort of secularism, in order to recognize the power of man, therefore ends up by doing without God and even by denying Him.

**Lapsed Catholics**  The second sphere is that of those who do not practice. Today there is a very large number of baptized people who for the most part have not formally renounced their baptism but who are entirely indifferent to it and not living in accordance with it. The phenomenon of the nonpracticing is a very ancient one in the history of Christianity; it is the result of a natural weakness, a profound inconsistency which we unfortunately bear deep within us. Today however it shows certain new characteristics. It is often the result of the uprooting typical of our time. It also springs from the fact that Christians live in close proximity with non-believers and constantly experience the effects of unbelief. Furthermore, the non-practicing Christians of today, more so than those of previous periods, seek to explain and justify their position in the name of an interior religion, of personal independence or authenticity.

**The Resistance of Atheists and Lapsed Catholics**  Thus we have atheists and unbelievers on the one side and those who do not practice on the other, and both groups put up a considerable resistance to evangelization. The resistance of the former takes the form of a certain refusal and an inability to grasp the new order of things, the new meaning of the world, of life and of history; such is not possible if one does not start from a divine absolute. The resistance of the second group takes the form of inertia and the slightly hostile attitude of the person who feels that he is one of the family, who claims to know it all and to have tried it all and who no longer believes it.

**Evangelization Is an Ecclesial Activity**  The observation that the Church has been sent out and given a mandate to evangelize the world should awaken in us two convictions. The first is this: evangelization is for no one an individual and isolated act; it is one that is deeply ecclesial. . . . From this flows the second conviction: if each individual evangelizes in the name of the Church, who herself does so by virtue of a mandate from the Lord, no evangelizer is the absolute master of his evangelizing action, with a discretionary power to carry it out in accordance with individualistic criteria and perspectives; he acts in communion with the Church and her pastors.

**Evangelization in the Family/Domestic Church**   The family has well deserved the beautiful name of "domestic Church." This means that there should be found in every Christian family the various aspects of the entire Church. Furthermore, the family, like the Church, ought to be a place where the Gospel is transmitted and from which the Gospel radiates.

In a family which is conscious of this mission, all the members evangelize and are evangelized. The parents not only communicate the Gospel to their children, but from their children they can themselves receive the same Gospel as deeply lived by them. And such a family becomes the evangelizer of many other families, and of the neighborhood of which it forms part.

**The Holy Spirit Is the Catalyst and Goal of Evangelization**
It must be said that the Holy Spirit is the principal agent of evangelization: it is He who impels each individual to proclaim the Gospel, and it is He who in the depths of consciences causes the word of salvation to be accepted and understood. But it can equally be said that He is the goal of evangelization: He alone stirs up the new creation the new humanity of which evangelization is to be the result, with that unity in variety which evangelization wishes to achieve within the Christian community. Through the Holy Spirit the Gospel penetrates to the heart of the world, for it is He who causes people to discern the signs of the times — signs willed by God — which evangelization reveals and puts to use within history.

**Evangelizing with Our Lives**   The world calls for and expects from us simplicity of life, the spirit of prayer, charity toward all, especially toward the lowly and the poor, obedience and humility, detachment and self-sacrifice. Without this mark of holiness, our word will have difficulty in touching the heart of modern man. It risks being vain and sterile.

**Truth at the Core of Evangelization**   The Gospel entrusted to us is also the word of truth. A truth which liberates and which alone gives peace of heart is what people are looking for when we proclaim the good news to them. The truth about God, about man and his mysterious destiny, about the world; the difficult truth that we seek in the Word of God and of which, we repeat, we are neither the masters nor the owners, but the depositaries, the heralds and the servants. Every evangelizer is expected to have a reverence for truth, especially since the truth that he studies and communicates is none other than revealed truth and hence, more than any other, a sharing in the first truth which is God Himself.

The preacher of the Gospel will therefore be a person who even at the price of personal renunciation and suffering always seeks the truth that he must transmit to others. He never betrays or hides truth out of a desire to please men, in order to astonish or to shock, nor for the sake of originality or a desire to make an impression. He does not refuse truth. He does not obscure revealed truth by being too idle to search for it, or for the sake of his own comfort, or out of fear. He does not neglect to study it. He serves it generously, without making it serve him.

**The Mandate to Evangelize**   Is it then a crime against others' freedom to proclaim with joy a good news which one has come to know through the Lord's mercy? It would be useful if every Christian and every evangelizer were to pray about the following thought: men can gain salvation also in other ways, by God's mercy, even though we do not preach the Gospel to them; but as for us, can we gain salvation if through negligence or fear or shame — what St. Paul called "blushing for the Gospel" — or as a result of false ideas we fail to preach it?

Let us therefore preserve our fervor of spirit. Let us preserve the delightful and comforting joy of evangelizing, even when it is in tears that we must sow. May it mean for us . . . an interior enthusiasm that nobody and nothing can quench.

## *Conclusion*

Evangelization means sharing the good news. It is a form of communication, and, as we have seen, *lectio divina* is an inspired model for such. Paul reminds us that evangelization begins with ourselves on an ongoing basis, however familiar we may be with the Gospel message. Because *lectio* is designed for personal and communal transformation it is quite fitting for such renewal and conversion.

The joy and energy underlying our evangelization efforts flows from the integrated graces of the Trinity: the creative providence of the Father, the redemption of humanity by Jesus, and the enlightenment and sustenance provided by the Spirit.

Evangelization means giving witness to Jesus and the Gospel in word and deed, of which Paul VI is an inspiring example. Just as he gave us a creed from which to understand our faith in modern terms, and a letter at the beginning of his pontificate setting its course by identifying dialogue as the Church's fundamental communications value, so he effectively winds down his pontificate by reflecting on the divine aspect of communications, how to receive and spread the good news in an enthusiastic and comprehensible way.

The simultaneously stand-alone and cohesive quality of this material is amenable to *lectio divina* in a manner similar to the Our Father. Each aspect of the message has its own meaning and significance that manifests an even greater fullness when taken as a whole.

Just as the Bible in its capacity as the word of God in human language requires proper interpretation and dissemination, so the core message of the Bible, the good news of Jesus, requires a synthesis of divine inspiration and providence and human effort in order to be effectively communicated. Paul the diplomat offers us a charter of evangelization founded on biblical guidance and pastoral wisdom and experience.

## Closing Prayer / Meditation

*Pope Paul's Prayer at Aldo Moro's Funeral Mass*
*The Basilica of St. John Lateran*
*May 13, 1978*

And now our lips, closed as if by an enormous obstacle, like the great stone rolled to the entrance of Christ's tomb, wish to open to express the "De profundis," that is, the cry and the weeping of the unutterable grief with which this tragedy suffocates our voice.

Lord, hear us!

And who can listen to our lament, if not You, O God of life and death? You did not hearken to our supplication for the safety of Aldo Moro, this good, meek, wise, innocent, and friendly man; but You, O Lord, have not abandoned his immortal spirit, sealed by Faith in Christ, who is the resurrection and the life. For him, for him.

Lord, hear us!

Grant, O God, Father of mercy, that there will not be interrupted communion which, even in the shadows of death, still exists between those who have departed from this temporal existence and ourselves still living in this day in which the sun inexorably sets. The program of our being as redeemed is not a vain one: our flesh will rise again, our life will be eternal! Oh! Let our faith match this promised reality right now. We will see them again, Aldo and all the living in Christ, blessed in the infinite God!

Lord, hear us!

And meanwhile, O Lord, grant that our heart, placated by the power of your Cross, may be able to forgive the unjust and mortal outrage inflicted on this beloved man and on those who suffered the same cruel fate. Grant that all of us may gather in the pure shroud of his noble memory the surviving heritage of his upright conscience, his human and cordial example, his dedication to the civil and spiritual redemption of the beloved Italian nation!

Lord, hear us!

Before the end of this rite of supplication in which we have prayed for the eternal peace of this brother of ours, we raise our arms to bless all those present in this Temple or those who, not having been able to find a place within its walls, have remained in the square, and also all those who, though distant, are united with us spiritually: in particular we intend to embrace with this paternal gesture of ours also those whose hearts are weighed down with agony and grief for some relative, the victim of such savage violence. Our afflicted prayer extends also to these victims. We invoke on everyone the strengthening assistance of the Lord, the bringer of serenity and hope.

# Suggested Resources

The most comprehensive biography of Paul VI in English is Peter Hebblethwaite's *Paul VI: The First Modern Pope* (Mahwah, N.J.: Paulist Press, 1993.) Hebblethwaite was a Vatican reporter who also wrote a highly praised biography of Paul's predecessor, Pope John XXIII.

Barrett, William E. *Shepherd of Mankind: A Biography of Pope Paul VI.* New York: Doubleday, 1964.

Clancy, John G. *Apostle for Our Time: Pope Paul VI.* London: Collins, 1963.

Gonzalez, J. L., and Mary F. Ingoldsby, trans. *Chats with Pope Paul.* Boston: Daughters of St. Paul, 1965.

Guitton, Jean. *The Pope Speaks: Dialogues of Paul VI with Jean Guitton.* New York: Meredith Press, 1968.

Hatch, Alden. *Pope Paul VI.* New York: Random House, 1966.

Hebblethwaite, Peter. *John XXIII.* London: Geoffrey Chapman, 1984.

————. *Paul VI: The First Modern Pope.* Mahwah, N.J.: Paulist Press, 1993.

O'Connor, Edward D., C.S.C., and Tom Bonaiuto, trans. *Pope Paul and the Spirit: Charisms and Church Renewal in the Teaching of Paul VI.* Notre Dame, Ind.: Ave Maria Press, 1978.

New York Times. *The Pope's Journey to the United States.* New York: Bantam Books, 1965.

Pallenberg, Corrado. *Pope Paul VI.* Toronto: Longmans Canada, 1968.

Paul VI, Pope. *Dialogues: Reflections on God and Man.* Trans. John G. Clancy. New York: Simon and Schuster, 1968.

————. *Good News for Married Love.* Trans. Randall Blackall. Collegeville, Minn.: Liturgical Press, 1974.

————. *Mary: God's Mother and Ours.* Boston: Daughters of St. Paul, 1979.

Walsh, James, S.J., ed. *The Mind of Paul VI: On the Church and the World.* Trans. Archibald Colquhoun. Milwaukee: Bruce Publishing Company, 1964.

Wigginton, F. Peter. *The Popes of Vatican Council II.* Chicago: Franciscan Herald Press, 1983.

United States Catholic Conference. *The Teachings of Pope Paul VI.* Washington, D.C.: USCC, 1968–73.

## Lectio Divina

Casey, Michael. *Sacred Reading: The Ancient Art of Lectio Divina.* Liguori, Mo.: Liguori/Triumph, 1995.

———. *Toward God: The Ancient Wisdom of Western Prayer.* Liguori, Mo.: Liguori/Triumph, 1996.

Guigo II. *The Ladder of Monks and Twelve Meditations.* Trans. Edmund Colledge and James Walsh. Kalamazoo, Mich.: Cistercian Publications, 1981.

Hall, Thelma. *Too Deep for Words: Rediscovering Lectio Divina.* Mahwah, N.J.: Paulist Press, 1988.

Keating, Thomas. *Invitation to Love.* Rockport, Mass.: Element Books, 1992.

Leclercq, Dom Jean. *The Love of Learning and the Desire for God.* New York: Mentor Omega Books, 1962.

Magrassi, Mariano. *Praying the Bible: An Introduction to Lectio Divina.* Collegeville, Minn.: Liturgical Press, 1998.

Masini, Mario. *Lectio Divina: An Ancient Prayer That Is Ever New.* Staten Island, N.Y.: Alba House, 1998.

McDonald, Patrick J., and Claudette M. McDonald. *Marital Spirituality.* Mahwah, N.J.: Paulist Press, 1999.

Miller, Charles E. *Together in Prayer: Learning to Love the Liturgy of the Hours.* Staten Island, N.Y.: Alba House, 1994.

Muto, Susan Annette. *A Practical Guide to Spiritual Reading.* Petersham, Mass.: St. Bede's Publications, 1994.

Pennington, M. Basil. *Lectio Divina: Renewing the Ancient Practice of Praying the Scriptures.* New York: Crossroad, 1998.

Shannon, William H. *Seeking the Face of God.* New York: Crossroad, 1990.

Toon, Peter. *The Art of Meditating on Scripture: Understanding Your Faith, Renewing Your Mind, Knowing Your God.* Grand Rapids, Mich.: Zondervan, 1993.

———. *Meditating upon God's Word.* London: Darton, Longman & Todd, 1988.

Vest, Norvene. *Bible Reading for Spiritual Growth.* New York: HarperCollins Publishers, 1993.

———. *No Moment Too Small.* Kalamazoo, Mich.: Cistercian Publications, 1994.

Wiederkehr, Macrina. *A Tree Full of Angels: Seeing the Holy in the Ordinary.* San Francisco: HarperCollins, 1988.

# Acknowledgments

This book has many contributors. First and foremost, I would like to thank my mother for providing me with a solid Catholic example, education, and formation, and for encouraging me in my spiritual journey and vocation. I am also grateful for the support received during the beginning of my formational and literary interest in Paul VI.

I am grateful to Big T for his continual love and support and the laughs and help he provided.

I thank Joan Cowen for her guidance and encouragement in my spiritual and vocational journey.

I thank Fr. Tim for his guidance, feedback, encouragement, and consistent support of my interest in Paul VI and this project.

I am grateful to Neal "The Commodore" Murphy for his friendship, feedback, and admiration of Paul VI, and for his ongoing enthusiastic evaluation and encouragement of my literary efforts.

I am thankful and fortunate to have worked with my editor, Roy M. Carlisle, whose editorial skills, suggestions, openness, experience, and support were integral to the pleasurable cultivation and completion of this project.

I am grateful to John Jones and Mike Egan for their facilitation of the publishing of this book through their confidence and their literary and spiritual foresight and openness.

To everyone else who contributed to this effort I extend my appreciation.

I thank Pope Paul VI for his witness, inspiration, and intercession. Grazie.

# About the Editor

Karl A. Schultz is the director of Genesis Personal Development Center in Pittsburgh, Pennsylvania. He gives presentations and retreats throughout the world on *lectio divina*, Pope Paul VI, and other biblical spirituality and personal growth subjects. His books along with audiotapes, CDs, and DVDs of his presentations can be ordered from Genesis Personal Development Center, 3431 Gass Avenue, Pittsburgh, PA 15212-2239. E-mail: *karlaschultz@juno.com*; website: *karlaschultz.com*; telephone: 412-766-7545.

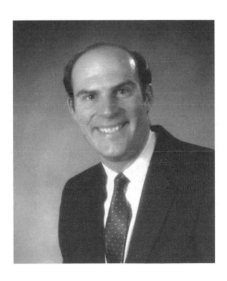

# Of Related Interest

**Walter Cardinal Kasper**
**LEADERSHIP IN THE CHURCH**
*How Traditional Roles Can Serve*
*the Christian Community Today*

This book offers a timely and profound look at the enduring meaning of church office, and the guidance it is called to provide in light of a changed world and a challenging future. Topics addressed include: the universal vs. local church; the ministry of the bishop, priest, and deacon; apostolic succession; and the practical application of canonical norms.

"In this new collection of essays Cardinal Kasper deals with crucial questions for the Church of our day. He combines the theoretical skills of a university professor with the practical wisdom of a residential bishop. Committed to the program and priorities of Vatican II, he writes with openness and moderation. Even theologians who might differ from some of his conclusions will be impressed by the strength of his arguments." — Avery Cardinal Dulles, S.J.

"Within these pages can be found some of the best contemporary Roman Catholic reflection on many of the most pressing challenges facing all the churches." — William G. Rusch

0-8245-1977-9, cloth

crossroad

# Of Related Interest

### Christoph Cardinal Schoenborn
### WITH JESUS EVERY DAY
*How Believing Transforms Living*

From his popular public addresses to his *New York Times* articles on evolution and faith, Cardinal Schoenborn has emerged as a worldwide figure in Catholic life. In *With Jesus Every Day*, Cardinal Schoenborn invites the reader to a deeper understanding of Jesus as Christ. He traces the life of Jesus and looks at how the faith was passed on and developed through the ages into our present time. With topics such as the voice of conscience, freedom in Christ, and acting responsibly, this book offers a clear and accessible presentation of the tradition of faith and the responses it gives for the basic questions of life.

ISBN 0-8245-2420-9, cloth

crossroad

# Of Related Interest

**Pope Benedict XVI**
**THE YES OF JESUS CHRIST**
*Spiritual Exercises in Faith, Hope, and Love*

Anyone wanting to understand Pope Benedict XVI's view of the relationship between Christianity and the world must read this eloquent book. Secular thought has failed to answer the great questions of human existence. Benedict XVI invites us to rediscover the Christ-centered basis for hope.

0-8245-2374-1, paperback

Check your local bookstore for availability.
To order directly from the publisher,
please call 1-800-707-0670 for Customer Service
or visit our Web site at *www.cpcbooks.com.*
For catalog orders, please send your request to the address below.

THE CROSSROAD PUBLISHING COMPANY
16 Penn Plaza, Suite 1550
New York, NY 10001

All prices subject to change.

crossroad